Firm Size, Innovation and Market Structure

1

NEW HORIZONS IN THE ECONOMICS OF INNOVATION

General Editor: Christopher Freeman, *Emeritus Professor of Science Policy,*
SPRU – Science and Technology Policy Research, University of Sussex, UK

Technical innovation is vital to the competitive performance of firms and of nations and
for the sustained growth of the world economy. The economics of innovation is an area
that has expanded dramatically in recent years and this major series, edited by one of
the most distinguished scholars in the field, contributes to the debate and advances in
research in this most important area.

The main emphasis is on the development and application of new ideas. The series
provides a forum for original research in technology, innovation systems and management,
industrial organization, technological collaboration, knowledge and innovation, research
and development, evolutionary theory and industrial strategy. International in its
approach, the series includes some of the best theoretical and empirical work from both
well-established researchers and the new generation of scholars.

Titles in the series include:

The Theory of Innovation
Entrepreneurs, Technology and Strategy
Jon Sundbo

The Emergence and Growth of Biotechnology
Experiences in Industrialised and Developing Countries
Rohini Acharya

Knowledge and Investment
The Sources of Innovation in Industry
Rinaldo Evangelista

Learning and Innovation in Economic Development
Linsu Kim

The Economics of Knowledge Production
Funding and the Structure of University Research
Aldo Geuna

Innovation and Research Policies
An International Comparative Analysis
Paul Diederen, Paul Stoneman, Otto Toivanen and Arjan Wolters

Learning and Knowledge Management in the Firm
From Knowledge Accumulation to Strategic Capabilities
Gabriela Dutrénit

Knowledge Spillovers and Economic Growth
Regional Growth Differentials across Europe
M.C.J. Caniëls

Successful Innovation
Towards a New Theory for the Management of Small and Medium-sized Enterprises
Jan Cobbenhagen

Firm Size, Innovation and Market Structure
The Evolution of Industry Concentration and Instability
Mariana Mazzucato

Firm Size, Innovation and Market Structure

The Evolution of Industry Concentration and Instability

Mariana Mazzucato

Open University, Milton Keynes, UK

NEW HORIZONS IN THE ECONOMICS OF INNOVATION

Edward Elgar

Cheltenham, UK • Northampton, MA, USA

Published by
Edward Elgar Publishing Limited
Glensanda House
Montpellier Parade
Cheltenham
Glos GL50 1UA
UK

Edward Elgar Publishing, Inc.
136 West Street
Suite 202
Northampton
Massachusetts 01060
USA

A catalog record for this book is available from the British Library

Library of Congress Cataloging in Publication Data

Mazzucato, Mariana, 1968–
    Firm size, innovation and market structure : the evolution of industry
concentration and instability / Mariana Mazzucato.
    (New horizons in the economics of innovation)
    Includes bibliographical references and index.
    1. Industrial organization (Economic theory) 2. Industries—Size—Computer
simulation. 3. Industrial concentration—Computer simulation. 4. Technological
innovations—Economic aspects—Computer simulation. 5. Evolutionary economics.
I. Title. II. Series.

HD2326 .M38 2000
338.6—dc21

                                                00–035347

ISBN 1 84064 346 3

Printed and bound in Great Britain by
Biddles Ltd, Guildford and King's Lynn

For Carlo

Contents

Figures

Tables

Acknowledgments

This book could not have been written without the help and encouragement provided to me by many people. I am very grateful to Duncan Foley for the long hours he spent with me when I was first learning computer simulation methods; to Willi Semmler and Lance Taylor for their helpful comments; to Yuri Yegorov for his suggestions on the first part of Chapter 2; to Steven Klepper for the large amount of time he put into revising Chapter 4; and to Paul Geroski for the interesting conversations on firm size dynamics during the past two years. A special thank you to Ernesto and Alessandra Mazzucato for their continuous presence and support.

Various chapters benefitted from the insightful feedback received from seminar and conference participants at the University of Augsburg; the Center for Research on Innovation and Competition (CRIC) in Manchester; the Maastricht Economic Research Institute on Innovation and Technology (MERIT); the Graduate Workshop in Computational Economics at the Santa Fe Institute; and the Technology and Economic Dynamics project at the International Institute for Applied Systems Analysis (IIASA). The last stages of preparation benefitted from a European Union Marie Curie Research Training Grant (contract no. ERBFMBICT972263). Finally, I thank the journals *Structural Change and Economic Dynamics* and the *Journal of Evolutionary Economics* for allowing articles to be reprinted here in Chapters 2 and 4, respectively, and the corresponding anonymous referees who commented on those two chapters. I, of course, bear sole responsibility for any errors in the book.

Introduction

The book uses evolutionary economic theory, non-linear dynamics and computer simulation techniques to explore a dynamic issue in industrial economics: the feedback between firm size, innovation and market structure. For many years, much theoretical and empirical research effort focussed on the effect of market structure on innovation, or on the effect of firm size on innovation, rather than on the feedback between the variables:

> The chain of causation is said to run from existing market structure to the pace of innovation, though it must be recognized at once that there are feedback effects from innovation to market structure. (Scherer and Ross, 1990, p. 630)

> A methodological problem common to almost all the studies of the relationship between size and innovation is that they overlook the effect of innovation on firm growth (and hence, ultimately firm size). It is curious that the endogeneity of firm size, central to Schumpeter's notion of creative destruction, has been neglected, while the simultaneity associated with creative destruction has been recognized in some studies of the relationship between innovation and market concentration. This lacuna probably reflects the profession's primitive understanding of the determination of the size and growth of firms, an area of research that has just recently been revived. (Cohen and Levin, 1989, p. 1070)

One of the main obstacles to the full exploration of this relationship has been the 'linearity' assumption permeating both the theoretical and the empirical tools: the theoretical work being constrained by the linear 'structure → conduct → performance' approach and the empirical work by linear (or linearizing) quantitative methods. Starting in the 1980s, the development of 'new industrial organization' theory (Jacquemin, 1987) and 'evolutionary economics' (Nelson and Winter, 1982) began to relax these constraints with more dynamic frameworks and tools for studying industrial change. New industrial organization theory achieved this (partially) by emphasizing the *non-linear* relationship between structure, conduct and performance, and evolutionary economics by emphasizing how market structure and firm size evolve endogenously from the dynamics of firm-specific innovation. As the more static theoretical framework was (is) accompanied by static quantitative tools, this more dynamic framework has given rise to new more dynamic quantitative methods in industrial organization, such as the use of non-linear mathematics and computer simulation techniques.

'Evolutionary' economics refers to the relatively new branch in economics which focusses on the co-evolution of mechanisms creating differences between economic agents (for example, consumers, technologies, firms, industries, countries), and mechanisms of selection which winnow in on those differences. The evolutionary perspective on market structure differs from the traditional neoclassical perspective for various reasons: first, inter-firm variety is not seen as a result of 'imperfections' in an otherwise perfectly competitive world (which can be described by a 'representative' agent), but rather as the outcome of a competitive process characterized by firm-specific capabilities and innovation activities; second, since the latter are a permanent characteristic of competition, there is no reason why variety should disappear, even in the *long run*; and third, patterns characterizing industry structure, such as the firm-size distribution and level of instability, are not constrained by notions of 'equilibrium' or 'optimality' but are instead understood as properties 'emerging' from interactions between heterogeneous agents. These interactions are characterized both by degrees of freedom at the firm level (which create the inter-firm diversity) and by structural properties at the industry level which constrain the degrees of freedom. The object of evolutionary economics is to study the co-evolution of the degrees of freedom and the structural constraints (Dosi, 1984).

Since the study of firm size, innovation and market structure inevitably leads to the study of *differences* in firm size and innovation capabilities between firms, the emphasis of evolutionary economics on the origin and evolution of *variety* between firms makes it a particularly useful framework for this research topic. Evolutionary economists make use of metaphors and mathematical techniques from the field of biology (for example, evolution, mutation, imitation), as opposed to the use of physics by traditional neoclassical economists (for example, steady-state equilibrium). For instance, the role of differences between firms in creating economic change is often modeled using replicator dynamics, borrowed from evolutionary biology, which posit a 'distance from mean dynamic': a firm's growth rate depends on how its efficiency characteristics differ from the industry (weighted) average. If there are no differences between firms, there is no economic change!

One of the main objectives of evolutionary economics in the field of industrial organization has been to study how different 'stylized facts', such as the skewed size distribution of firms across a wide variety of industries, emerge from the interactions between firms which differ in attributes such as their innovation capabilities (see: Dosi et al., 1995; Klepper, 1996; Malerba and Orsenigo, 1996; Silverberg et al., 1988). The present book continues this particular line of investigation.

Chapter 1 reviews how classical (Smith, Ricardo, Marx), neoclassical and evolutionary perspectives in economics differ in their view of variety and order, and the implications of such differences for theories of firm size and market structure. It then reviews static, dynamic and stochastic theories of market structure: static theories emphasize the mechanism by which an optimal firm size emerges from profit maximization subject to a U-shaped average cost curve; dynamic theories emphasize the evolution over time of firm-specific learning and innovation capabilities; and stochastic theories emphasize the effect of idiosyncratic events on firm growth patterns. To better understand the dynamic and stochastic perspectives, the chapter outlines the interwoven relationship between micro interactions and emergent macro patterns, behind the role of firm-, industry- and technology-specific factors in influencing the empirical relationship between firm size, innovation and market structure. Given the dynamic relationships described in the theoretical and empirical work, the last section of the chapter reviews the usefulness of specific methods in non-linear dynamics (for example, replicator dynamics, master equations) and computer simulation techniques for exploring such complexity.

In Chapter 2 an evolutionary model is developed which studies how different types of feedback embodied in *dynamic* returns to scale, that is, the relationship between firm size and innovation, result in particular firm-size distributions and degrees of market share instability. Through the use of replicator dynamics and computer simulation techniques, the model studies the standard equilibrium results first for static returns to scale (the effect of size on the *direction* of costs) and then for dynamic returns to scale (the effect of size on the *rate* of cost reduction). In the static case, well-known results are found: decreasing returns to scale leads to a unique equilibrium and increasing returns to scale leads to multiple equilibria. In the dynamic case, less intuitive results emerge. We review these here briefly.

The model of dynamic returns to scale developed in Chapter 2 consists of a replicator equation which links the market share of each firm to its relative level of efficiency (costs), and an equation which links the firm's rate of cost reduction (that is, innovation) to its size. 'Positive feedback' describes the case where large firms are better innovators (faster rate of cost reduction) and 'negative feedback' where small firms are better innovators. The model is kept simple so that a clear typology can be made linking different market structures to variations in empirically relevant parameters. The parameters include the type of feedback between costs and shares (positive or negative), the initial distribution of firm efficiencies, and the industry average speed of cost reduction. The main results are: (1) with a very fast (slow) industry average speed of cost reduction, positive feedback between firm size and innovation leads to a competitive (monopolistic) market structure and asymptotic firm ranking is always *predictable* from initial efficiency levels; and (2) while negative feedback is characterized by the same results as positive feedback in the case when the industry average speed of cost reduction is either very fast or very slow, when it is instead at an intermediate level, negative feedback leads to *instability* in market shares and *unpredictability* in firm ranking. This last result indicates that not all types of negative feedback lead to unique predictable outcomes and hence that negative feedback should not be ignored by economists interested in disequilibrium dynamics. The results provide new insights on the dynamic implications of different qualitative and empirical studies regarding firm size, innovation and market instability (*qualitative studies*: Abernathy and Wayne, 1974; Klein, 1977; Woo and Cooper, 1982; *empirical studies*: Comanor, 1967; Geroski, 1990; Klepper, 1996; Lunn, 1986; Scherer, 1984).

Chapter 3 explores the effect of idiosyncratic and random events on the relationship between firm size and innovation. An idiosyncratic event might be the unique personality of a Chief Executive Officer, the trial and error aspect of innovation, or the (random) result of an advertising campaign. However, unlike some stochastic models which make firm size solely a result of random factors (for example, models based on Gibrat's law), the model retains the structural element embodied in the dynamic returns to scale studied in Chapter 2, and explores the degree to which shocks alter these deterministic results under different parameter configurations. The main results are: (1) positive feedback with shocks still leads to a concentrated market structure, but the *process* towards concentration is much more turbulent and final firm ranking unpredictable; and (2) stochastic shocks have more of an impact on market structure in (i) periods of *negative* feedback; (ii) in industries or periods characterized by an 'intermediate' level of technological opportunity; and (iii) when shocks are neither very large nor very small.

While Chapters 2 and 3 concentrate on modeling market concentration and market share instability, Chapter 4 asks whether instability at the production level is related to instability at the financial level (stock price volatility). Different empirical and theoretical contributions (including those found in Chapters 2 and 3) have found market share instability to be tied to industry-specific factors: instability is higher in the early phase of the industry life-cycle and in industries characterized by high entry, low capital intensity, high product innovation and high uncertainty. In the finance literature, the *excess volatility* of stock prices, that is, the much larger volatility of stock prices than dividends, has been tied to general economy-wide characteristics of investors (for example, animal spirits, herd behavior, self-fulfilling prophecies) instead of to industry-specific factors (Campbell and Shiller, 1988; Shiller, 1989). The chapter asks whether there is a relationship between market share instability and stock price volatility and to what degree this relationship is connected to industry-specific factors. To do so, it empirically explores one particular industry, the US automobile industry, for which detailed data regarding market shares, earnings and stock prices is available from 1900 onwards. Given the industry-specific nature of market share instability, an empirical relationship between market share instability and excess volatility could suggest that while over-reaction of investors explains the *existence* of excess volatility, industry-specific factors contribute to the *degree* of excess volatility. Since neither life-cycle nor finance theories attack this problem directly, the chapter uses insights from both approaches to build hypotheses which guide the data analysis. The empirical results suggest that the degree of excess volatility is indeed partly affected by industry-specific factors.

1. Firm-size dynamics: new ideas and dynamic methods

1 INTRODUCTION: VARIETY, ORDER AND COMPLEXITY

Firm-size dynamics have long been at the center of economic analysis, both at the level of the industry and of the economy as a whole. One of the principal features that distinguishes how this topic has been treated by different schools of thought is the way in which differences between firms (variety) and competition between firms (selection) are treated.

1.1 Variety

In traditional microeconomic theory, differences between firms arise due to 'imperfections' in the competitive mechanism. These include factors such as imperfect information, short-run technological rents and monopoly power. Since these factors are responsible for the imperfections in competition, it follows that the underlying 'true' nature of competition can be defined independently of them. The terms 'long run', to describe some sort of *natural* perfect state, and 'short run', to describe the system during its *transition* to that state, arises from this conception. Once supply and demand have adjusted and profit-maximizing firms have been able to update their expectations, diversity disappears.

In classical economic theory, as well as in more recent Schumpeterian 'evolutionary' economics, the competitive process is viewed not as a process which destroys differences, but as one which endogenously generates differences in firm capabilities and performances. Both approaches view competition as a *disequilibrium* process, in which firms constantly face the pressure to differentiate themselves in order to survive. In *Capital* (1919), Marx explicitly outlines how the process of competition forces firms to invest in cost-reducing innovation in order to decrease prices and increase market share. He claims that since firms embody different innovation strategies, turnover times and capital–labor ratios, competition necessarily generates inter-firm differences in profit rates, costs and market shares. In this view, variety between firms is the *result* of competition and it is when competition is *not* present that there are no differences between firms.

Schumpeter describes innovation not only as an essential factor in capitalist competition, but also as a complicated process guided by entrepreneurial decisions and actions which cannot be abstracted from when studying the competitive process. He claimed that perfect competition is not only unrealistic, but that even if it did exist it would not be optimal because: (1) perfect information will prevent firms from investing in technological change since they cannot reap the associated rents, and (2) small firms will often not have the large funds needed for investment in research and development (R&D) (Schumpeter, 1942). Thus a homogeneous world would have a devastating effect on the growth of gross domestic product (GDP)! The idea that novelty continually emerges from the evolution of the system, is incompatible with the concepts of optimization and prediction so fundamental to neoclassical economics:

> A system ... that at every point in time fully utilizes its possibilities to its best advantage may yet in the long run be inferior to a system that does so at no given point in time, because the latter's failure to do so may be a condition for the level of speed of long-run performance. (Schumpeter, 1942, p. 83)

The evolutionary perspective emphasizes the ability of firms to alter their market position and, in the presence of strong increasing returns to scale, to alter the structure of the market significantly. Firm actions are not assumed to be optimal rational responses to a given set of prices but are instead analysed as 'routines' or 'rules of thumb' which agents use to adapt to a complex environment. The fact that agents have different cognitive structures, experiences and habits means that they will also have different routines, and this is one of the main sources of inter-firm variety. In describing the strategic actions undertaken by firms, modern writers in this tradition focus on the firm-, technology- and industry-specific conditions which both create and limit variety. Since industries are characterized by different types of technological opportunity (ease of innovation), appropriability (ease of capturing rents), cumulativity (ease of maintaining current leadership positions) and knowledge-base conditions (tacit versus codifiable), we can expect there to be a soft relationship between firm behavior and structural conditions as opposed to a unique behavioral theory which holds for all firms (Pavitt, 1984).

Following Schumpeter, the main factor identified by evolutionary economics as leading to *long-run* differences in performance variables is technological change. Diversity is both a precondition and a result of innovation:

> Its (technical change) precondition and outcome are varying degrees of appropriability of the innovation and differential profitabilities. This very process, however,

provides both the incentive and the need for other firms to imitate and/or undertake further innovation. (Dosi and Orsenigo, 1988, p. 27)

Variety, however, is limited because of the evolutionary forces of selection which allow only some firms to survive and grow. Since which firms survive is an outcome both of the selection mechanism and of initial chance events (especially in the presence of increasing returns), it is not possible to claim that the end result is 'optimal'.

1.2 Different Notions of 'Order': Equilibrium, Centers of Gravity, Regularities

The emphasis on variety in evolutionary economics does not imply a lack of 'order'. In fact, in both classical and evolutionary economics, competition is viewed as a process characterized simultaneously by disequilibrium and by order: by 'chance' and by 'necessity'. The concept of order, however, is different from the neoclassical concept of 'equilibrium'.

An equilibrium firm size in neoclassical economics emerges from the underlying assumption on technology and firm behavior, that is, the U-shaped average cost curve and profit maximization. Once price-taking firms experience diseconomies of scale, they will stop expanding, so that in the long run, the equilibrium size of all firms is predictable. Equilibrium is associated with an optimal value which maximizes social welfare (for example, consumer surplus).

The classicals stress the way in which differences between firms revolve around a competitive 'center of gravity' which can be defined independently of the variety itself. Adam Smith, David Ricardo and Karl Marx all maintained that inter-firm and inter-industry differences will always exist, but that there will also be tendencies towards 'natural' levels of certain variables. Marx claims that although intra-industry differences in costs, size and profits will persist in the long run, the movement of capital towards the industry with higher profit rates will create a tendency for inter-industry profit rates to equalize. Although each industry is characterized by a wide variety of firms (consistent with the evolutionary perspective), it is the 'regulating capital' in each industry, that is, the firm using the 'best socially available technique', that serves as a target for capital mobility. Another example of the concept of center of gravity in classical economics is the idea that although market prices at any point in time might not equal 'prices of production' (prices corresponding to labor values), they do revolve around them. Smith writes:

The natural price ... is, as it were, the central price, to which the prices of all commodities are continually gravitating. Different accidents may sometimes keep them suspended a good deal above it, and sometimes force them down somewhat below it. But whatever may be the obstacles which hinder them from settling in this center of repose and continuance, they are constantly tending towards it. (Smith, 1937, p. 65)

The combination of a regulating force (for example, inter-industry equalization of profit rates) and of a disequilibrating force (for example, intra-industry profit-rate differences), is clearly explained in the quotation by Smith, which refers to the effect of the industry life-cycle on industry profit rates:

> The establishment of any manufacture or any new branch of commerce, or of any new practice in agriculture, is always a speculation from which the projector promises himself extraordinary profits. These profits sometimes are very great and sometimes, more frequently, perhaps, they are quite otherwise; but in general, they bear no regular proportion to those of other trades in the neighborhood. If the project succeeds, they are commonly at first very high. When the trade or practice becomes thoroughly established, and well known, the competition reduces them to the level of other trades. (Smith, 1937, p. 131)

The emphasis of the classicals on 'centers of gravitation' and laws of motion, does not mean that economic phenomena can be predicted *ex ante*, but rather that there are *constraints* imposed on economic agents which arise from the nature of the regulating forces. In Marx, it is the *source* of profits in the capitalist 'mode of production' which causes value to be regulated by abstract labor. It is only those constraints, and not the exact actions, that can be (partially) known *ex ante*. Changes in the centers of gravity (for example, direct and indirect labor requirements) are determined by changes in the structure of production which, being regulated by the dynamics of accumulation and technical change, are in continuous change themselves (Semmler, 1984). Furthermore, the center of gravity is not associated with an 'optimal' outcome but a 'necessary' one, where the necessity emerges from the constraints.

In evolutionary economics, variety among firm characteristics does not revolve around a core that is independent of the variety, but instead produces 'regularities' which *emerge* directly from the variety itself. The macro config-uration which emerges from the interaction of heterogeneous agents, influences the micro-level interaction:

> The dynamics of an industry can be represented as the process of self-organization whereby technology, structures and behavior interact to produce relatively ordered evolutionary paths ... while in turn the evolving morphology of the system feeds back on the capabilities, incentives, constraints and behaviors of individual agents. (Dosi and Orsenigo, 1987, p. 15)

For example, the empirical regularity of a skewed size distribution of firms has been modeled in evolutionary economics as an outcome of a dynamic process in which firm imitation and innovation activities affect market structure, and market structure in turn affects innovation (Silverberg et al., 1988). Many of the empirical regularities reviewed in Section 2 owe their findings to researchers in this tradition. It is the focus on the co-evolution of (emergent) structure and firm heterogeneity that most characterizes this approach:

> The patterns of evolution of the system are determined by the interaction between structural constraints (such as technological asymmetries between firms) and behavioral degrees of freedom of each economic agent ... our model will focus on the evolving relationship between the range of possible performance outcomes and the nature of structural constraints. (Dosi, 1984, p. 11)

As in classical economics, the notion of 'order' in evolutionary economics is not associated with any notion of 'optimality', as it is in neoclassical economics. For example, the empirical regularity of a skewed size distribution of firms, which much work in this tradition has attempted to model and explain, is not necessarily optimal.

1.3 Complexity

The relationship described above between structural constraints and degrees of freedom, is similar to the feedback between 'chance' and 'necessity' referred to in modern theories of complexity (Santa Fe Institute, 1990). The term 'complexity' arises from the Greek root 'plex', which means 'to weave'. Complexity refers to the qualitative richness which arises when variables are inter-woven and when their interaction creates an entity or pattern very different from the simple addition of the parts, and which itself affects the interaction of the parts.

Studies focussing on technological change face the issue of complexity since firm-specific patterns of technological change cause changes in market structure, which in turn cause changes in the patterns of technological change (reviewed in Section 4, below). The *cumulative* aspect of innovation, where 'size begets size', causes industrial dynamics to be characterized by non-linear and path-dependent processes, where early (random) events have lasting and irreversible effects on the evolution of the system (Arthur, 1989; David, 1985, 1994; Krugman, 1979; Rosenberg, 1963). It is for this reason that the evolutionary paradigm has insisted on developing alternative quantitative tools in economics. Linear (or linearizing) econometric techniques and closed-form mathematical solutions have difficulty in capturing the rich and complex dynamics embodied in evolutionary processes. Different types of techniques in non-linear mathematics (for example, Lotka–Volterra equations, master equations, replicator dynamics) and computer simulation methods have proved promising in the exploration of such complex systems (Nelson, 1995; Foley, 1997). We review some of these methods in Section 6, below.

Whereas a critique of some evolutionary work in economics has been that it over-emphasizes the random and history dependent nature of change, a critique to the classical methodology has been that it focusses too much on the deterministic (tendential) laws of order, ignoring the effects of different types of firm-specific behavior on the 'laws' regulating economic change (Dosi, 1984). At the center of the discussion lies the question of how to define the long run in a system whose micro properties are in continuous change, and whose interactive properties have qualitative effects on the macro configuration which emerges. Dosi (1984), Dosi and Kaniovski (1994) and Iwai (1984a, b) develop different frameworks in which there is feedback between 'laws' and random events (for example, entry decisions). Iwai clearly describes this alternative conception:

> The long run must be viewed at best as a statistical steady-state which is maintained by offsetting motions of a large number of firms alternately winning and losing the competitive struggles for technological superiority. This statistical steady-state is, in other words, a microscopic disequilibria ... Profits in excess of the normal rate are still the sign of disequilibria but disequilibrium is no longer the synonym for the short-run ... The short run can no longer be treated as a mere fleeting moment in a smooth adjustment towards equilibrium but as a solid reality which has its own law of motion. (Iwai, 1990, p. 20)

Dosi et al. (1997b) develop a model with heterogeneous agents and continuous stochastic entry which produces certain long-run properties (limit properties of the size distribution of firms), which they claim is a 'vindication' of the intuition of classical economists that conditions of entry and variety in techniques of production can determine centers of gravity around which actual variables fluctuate.

The rest of the chapter will discuss issues regarding the complex relationship between firm size, innovation and market structure, and propose some alternative techniques which can be used for studying such complexity. The co-evolution of structural factors and random (local) factors are both emphasized. Section 2 motivates the discussion by presenting empirical 'regularities' in industrial dynamics which make an 'evolutionary' view of change particularly relevant; Section 3 reviews theoretical explanations of these regularities by linking cost theory to theories of firm size, specifying the limits of static analysis; Section 4 continues the discussion concerning dynamic cost analysis with an empirical look at the feedback between firm size and innovation; Section 5 provides a summary; and finally, Section 6 introduces some new quantitative techniques which attempt to address the novel and 'complex' aspects of the ideas introduced in Sections 3 and 4.

2 STYLIZED FACTS REGARDING FIRM-SIZE DYNAMICS

The following 'stylized facts' have made the relationship between firm size and innovation central to the study of industrial dynamics:

- Firm-size distributions in real industries often look like a Pareto, Yule or log-normal distribution (Ijiri and Simon, 1977; Sutton, 1997). The exact patterns vary across industries and between different stages of the industry life-cycle (Klepper, 1996).
- The 'industry life-cycle' has been identified as a recognizable pattern in many industries. The early stage is characterized by market share instability and a relatively competitive market structure; the mature stage is characterized by relatively stable market shares and a more concentrated market structure (Abernathy and Utterback, 1975; Klein 1977; Klepper, 1996). Innovation by small firms has been found to be more prevalent in the early stage of the life-cycle (Acs and Audretsch, 1990).
- Within industries, there is long-run persistence of variety in techniques, costs and profitabilities across firms (Mueller, 1986, 1990).
- Firms differ systematically in their commitment to innovation and their ability to innovate. Innovation in products and processes is largely endogenous to the activity of the firm, via R&D activities, learning by doing/using, and capital–labor relations. This makes market structures endogenous to the process of innovation (Dosi et al., 1988).
- 'Vigorous' innovation has been found to lead to more competitive market structures, and radical innovation has been found to be more character-istic of small firms than large firms (Geroski, 1990; Gort and Konakayama, 1982; Lunn, 1986).
- Learning by doing and other forms of increasing returns to scale, create lock-in dynamics which allow some firms and industries to grow persis-tently more than others (Arthur, 1989; David, 1985; Klepper, 1996).

These regularities have caused serious questioning of the neoclassical theory of firm size. Traditional analysis tends to emphasize the role of economies of scale in determining the optimal size of a firm. In this view, diseconomies of scale lead to competitive equilibria with similar market shares, and economies of scale lead to a very concentrated market structure where a few large firms dominate the industry. Yet the persistence of differences between firms (in size, costs, profits, innovation) and the periodic increases in market share instability have caused new approaches to emerge which emphasize more dynamic, sometimes stochastic, factors affecting industry market structure.

3 THE THEORY OF MARKET STRUCTURE AND THE MEASUREMENT OF COMPETITION

Theories of firm growth and market structure can be divided into three approaches: (1) a static approach which emphasizes the optimal allocation of scarce factors of production, where an optimum firm size emerges from the underlying cost dynamics; (2) a stochastic approach which emphasizes the idiosyncratic nature of firm growth patterns, and (3) a dynamic approach which emphasizes technological change and other forms of increasing returns to scale. The stochastic approach arose because of industrial economists' dissatisfaction with the strong behavioral assumptions underlying the traditional (static) theory of optimal firm size. The dynamic approach arose because of the lack of insight that the other two approaches provide on the role of firm- and industry-specific factors in producing increasing returns to scale. We review these below.

3.1 Static Cost Curve Analysis

In microeconomics, the size of firms is explained through the analysis of profit-maximizing behavior subject to increasing and decreasing returns to scale. We call this approach 'static' because of its emphasis on *given* production possibilities, in contrast to a 'dynamic' theory where the emphasis is on the discovery of *new* techniques and organizations of production and on the non-linear feedback between costs and market structure. Another reason why we call the traditional analysis 'static' is due to the linear relation posited between the structure of the market, the conduct of firms and the performance of firms. In this view, knowledge of the initial market structure provides sufficient information for the prediction of the price and quantity decisions of firms: if the market structure is oligopolistic, prices will be higher than marginal costs, and market shares will be larger than those in a competitive market. This will be distinguished below from a more dynamic approach in which there are feedback loops between structure, conduct and performance.

An equilibrium firm size emerges from the assumption of a U-shaped average cost curve: as long as average costs do not decline for ever, a limit is posed on the size of the firm. How many firms can co-exist in a market depends on whether the minimum efficient scale of production, at which all attainable unit cost savings are realized, is large or small in relation to the demand for an industry's output. This in turn depends on factors regarding the underlying technology and market.

Haldi and Whitcomb (1967) test various cost functions empirically, using a geometric relation between material required and capacity, and find little evidence for the case of decreasing returns to scale. The function tested was

$C = aX^b$, with $b > 0$ signifying increasing returns to scale, $b < 0$ signifying decreasing returns to scale, and $b = 0$ signifying constant returns to scale. They found economies of scale to be especially strong due to the ability of firms to expand all equipment uniformly, to break bottlenecks, to change techniques and to use multiplant operations. This is less true when there are inputs, such as managerial talents, which cannot easily be duplicated in production. The authors found that diseconomies of scale often arise from the exhaustion of managerial capabilities as the size of firms increase.

Stigler (1958) proposes an interesting perspective on firm size: the 'survivor technique'. He claims that the optimal size of a firm is only known *ex post* via those firm sizes that survive the competitive process. He finds that the size of the survivors depends on the particular technology used in the industry, the particular period in the business cycle, and the particular size class of firms. For example, he found that with steel ingots, increasing returns to scale lasted only up to a certain point, and with automobiles, large firms experienced decreasing returns to scale during inflationary periods and increasing returns to scale during other periods. To better understand the wide range of optimum firm sizes, he conducted an inter-industry study where he used different variables describing the role of advertising, the degree of vertical and horizontal integration, and the number of technical experts employed. He found that advertising and the capital/sales ratio were relatively insignificant in determining firm size, while the size of the plant and the relative number of engineers were highly significant. Williamson (1985) questioned why average costs should ever rise, since as long as firms can make contracts between legally separate units, the individual units can sign contracts in which they make use of common costly resources.

Sraffa (1926) and Young (1928), and to a certain extent Marshall (1948), were the first to write on the serious problems which neoclassical theory, and its attachment to concepts of equilibrium, runs into under conditions of monotonic increasing returns to scale. In general, all these arguments suggest that without a U-shaped average cost curve there is no longer an equilibrium size of the firm, causing price theory itself to be indeterminate. Yet when trying to understand the empirical regularities listed in Section 2 above the analysis of increasing returns to scale and the associated monopoly power do not seem to provide sufficient explanatory tools. The following statement by Kaldor still holds:

> We do not really know the causes of the uniformity in pattern which emerged in the last 50 years, under which not more than three large firms accounts for the great majority of total sales (perhaps 70–80% of the total or more) while the remainder is divided among a large number of small firms (normally several hundreds). This pattern emerged in some many different industries – like manufactures of automobiles and other durable consumer goods such as vacuum cleaners, refrigerators, electric light bulbs, or even newspapers or advertising agencies – that there must be some explanation in the dynamics of competition that goes beyond the considerations

usually taken into account. Clearly, increasing returns to scale has in a broad sense something to do with it, but that cannot be the whole explanation, since the numbers seem to be similar in countries as different as the United States or Switzerland. One may find (I am putting this as a hypothesis) that the leading producers have the same market share in both countries, even though the size of the market is 20 to 30 times as large in one case as in the other. (Kaldor, 1985, p. 53)

In reviewing dynamic cost theory below, we outline modern versions of this critique where emphasis is given to the emergence of multiple equilibria, and the process by which 'size begets size' allows 'small' initial events to have a critical role in determining future leaders (Arthur, 1989; David, 1994).

3.2   Dynamic Cost Curve Analysis

The more dynamic factors in cost curve analysis have to do with factors that affect costs not through static resource allocation, but through the exploration of new methods of production. The causation between the structure of the market, the conduct of firms and the performance of firms does not move in only one direction, but is instead characterized by different feedback loops (Jacquemin, 1987).

Dynamic cost analysis focusses on the ability of firms to decrease their costs, either through a classical learning curve, or through more complex innovation activities. The learning curve relates unit costs to accumulated volume. External economies that arise from learning curve dynamics allow those production processes that have longer production lengths to reap stronger increasing returns. The role of these external economies increases with market size, causing disadvantages to occur for industries (and countries) with smaller markets. In the presence of this dynamic, the short-run output decision is an investment decision which makes it necessary for the firm to go beyond the short-run profit-maximizing level of output. The optimal output path of the firm is one in which at each moment in time, short-run profits equal the present value of the total cost reduction which will be carried out in future periods by an additional unit of output at time t. The learning curve creates entry barriers and advantages to early starters and those who are able to achieve large market shares. Although the cost advantages are only temporary, they can have strong effects on profits and market shares when costs decline *rapidly*. In modeling learning curve dynamics, Spence (1981) found that if learning is either very slow or very fast, competition prevails because the entry barriers are low, while if learning is at a medium level, there are significant differences in inter-firm unit costs, depending on the time of entry. The model developed in Chapter 2 (Mazzucato, 1998) finds a similar result concerning the speed of learning.

The study of learning curve dynamics is related to new approaches to the study of increasing returns to scale and path-dependency. Arthur (1989) and

David (1985) develop models that look at how in the presence of increasing returns, early (random) events can affect choice of technique, plant location and asymptotic market structure. Due to the cumulative nature of technological change, firms that discover new technologies are able to maintain their lead even after the particular technology is obsolete (Landes, 1969; Rosenberg, 1963). This is especially true if network externalities cause consumers and other firms to 'lock into' a particular technology so that even if a new technology appears, it may not be adopted. Examples include the often cited stories of the Qwerty keyboard and the domination of VHS over Beta video-cassette recorders (David, 1985). Under such conditions, early events can have a strong and permanent effect on industry structure. The argument is well summarized by Arthur:

> In many parts of the economy, stabilizing forces appear not to operate. Instead positive feedback magnifies the effects of small economic shifts: the economic models that describe such effects differ vastly from the conventional ones. Diminishing returns imply a single equilibrium point for the economy, but positive feedback – increasing returns – makes for many possible equilibrium points. There is no guarantee that the particular economic outcome selected from among the many alternatives will be the 'best one.' Furthermore, once random economic events select a particular path, the choice may become locked-in regardless of the advantages of the alternatives. If one product or nation in a competitive market place gets ahead by 'chance,' it tends to stay ahead and even increase its lead. Predictable, shared markets are no longer guaranteed. (Arthur, 1990, p. 1)

Abernathy and Wayne (1974) review the reasons why strategies based on the learning curve are not appropriate during periods of market uncertainty (caused by sudden changes in demand and technology). In such situations, firms are better off dedicating their resources to 'exploration' activities rather than to 'exploitation' (for example, cost reduction through the increase of volume). They cite the period in the history of the US automobile industry (1926–30) when Ford's failure to adapt to changing demand conditions and its insistence on sticking with its old successful cost-reduction strategy of 'mass production', allowed General Motors (GM) to jump to first position in market share, a lead it never lost:

> In its effort to keep reducing Model T costs while wages were rising, Ford continued to invest heavily in plant, property, and equipment ... In the meantime, the market was changing. In the early 1920's, consumer demand began shifting to heavier, closed body and to more comfort. Ford's chief rival, General Motors, quickly responded to this shift with new designs. When costs could not be reduced as fast as they were added through design changes, the experience curve formula became inoperative. While this sequence should give pause to managers who wish to apply the experience curve to make product-line changes, it does not invalidate the principle of the learning curve, which assumes a standardized product. (Abernathy and Wayne, 1974, p. 115)

One could argue that GM was able to stay ahead due to the fact that it later decentralized production (with the development of the Pontiac, Buick, Cadillac and so on) to avoid the diseconomies of scale experienced by Ford.

Klein (1977) associates the difference between exploitation and exploration with the difference between static and dynamic efficiency. Static efficiency refers to those choices a firm makes along a given production possibilities frontier, such as an engineer who determines inputs and technology which enable a firm to produce output at minimal cost. There is no uncertainty here since the agent acts as though knowledge is already given; a rational agent plans on the basis of existing conditions. Dynamic efficiency instead refers to the extension of this frontier by exploiting as fully as possible a technological potential, such as an engineer who while trying to determine why a certain technique does not work as predicted, ends up making a new discovery. Here there is great uncertainty and the optimal tradeoffs cannot be known a priori. If knowledge can be improved, an agent acting on the basis of perfect knowledge is behaving *irrationally*. Klein claims that the ability of organizations to deal with uncertainty is a function of internal characteristics such as: (1) the diversity of its members (backgrounds and personality), and (2) the diversity of interactions between members and between members and the environment. In his study of changes in firm size and market instability in the automobile, aircraft, semiconductor and television industries, Klein (1977) claims that when technology and markets are still evolving, market shares tend to be more unstable and less concentrated because when exploration activities are more important than exploitation activities, it is easier for (flexible) newcomers to beat incumbents

The work by Abernathy and Wayne (1974) and Klein (1977) is related to the more recent literature on 'technological discontinuities' and 'architectural innovation'. Tushman and Anderson (1986) show that while 'competence-destroying' discontinuities are initiated by new firms and are associated with increased environmental turbulence, 'competence-enhancing' discontinuities are initiated by existing firms and are associated with decreased environmental turbulence. In a similar vein, Henderson and Clark (1990) show that architectural innovation (innovations that change the way in which the components of a product are linked together while leaving intact the core design concepts) tends to destroy the lead of established firms since it destroys the information-processing procedures that established firms are often locked into. Studies by Markides (1998), Hamel (1998) and Christensen (1997) also link industry turbulence and firm size with the type of change that a particular innovation introduces.

In recent years, the analysis of learning in economics has gone beyond the concept of the learning curve and been tied to the concept of 'organizational routines' (Nelson and Winter, 1982; March, 1991; Marengo, 1993; Winter,

1984). Firms can either learn to do better what they are already doing (exploitation) or try to learn new ways of doing things and new things to do (exploration). The tradeoff is sometimes postulated as one between 'efficiency' and 'flexibility'. The inability to 'mutate' when environmental conditions call for it, is a result of firm *inertia*. Inertia might arise from firms becoming 'satisfied' with their relatively high level of efficiency and market share, becoming less driven to explore new ways to reduce costs and increase quality (Simon, 1984). On the other hand, too much exploration can be risky since useless and bad information is costly, and since it may lead to the inability to exploit good discoveries when they are found, hence rendering little profit.

The analysis of firm 'routines' also exemplifies the tradeoff described above. On the one hand routines allow firms to adapt better to an uncertain and changing environment by learning from habits and mistakes. On the other hand they can cause organizational rigidity in times of needed mutation. Hannan and Freeman (1989) state:

> We think that it is a reasonable first approximation to think of organizations as possessing relatively fixed repertoires of highly reproducible routines. ... Our argument is that resistance to structural change is a likely by product of the ability to reproduce a structure with high-fidelity: high levels of reproducibility of structure imply strong inertial pressures. ... Such specialization limits the range of information about the environment that an organization can obtain and process. (Hannan and Freeman, 1989, p. 69)

Mutation is especially needed in times of uncertainty, like when demand and technology are changing rapidly. Uncertainty tends to differ between industries and between different periods in the life of an industry. The analysis of the life-cycle is particularly relevant to a dynamic analysis of competition. During the early stage of an industry's history, when entry rates are high and the product and market are uncertain, the flexibility of small new firms allows them to be the main sources of cost reduction and innovation (causing high rates of entry). This 'trial and error' stage is characterized by relatively more product innovation rather than process innovation. A 'shakeout' tends to occur after the price of the product has fallen (causing price–cost margins to fall) and economies of scale have set in. More stable product design and market demand allow larger firms to reap economies of scale and concentrate more on process innovation. High costs of R&D and the importance of process innovation strengthens the position of large firms and causes concentration to rise (Abernathy and Utterback, 1975; Acs and Audretsch, 1990; Klepper, 1996).

Dynamic theories which emphasize the *evolution* of market structure (as opposed to equilibrium properties of the asymptotic structure) require dynamic indices of competition to replace static indices which focus on the level of concentration at one period of time. Issues of theory and measurement are not unrelated:

> One of the chief objections to 'concentration ratios' as descriptions of market structure is that high ratios may be consistent with considerable instability in the market shares of individual firms. In judging the intensity of competition in an industry, the ability of leading firms to maintain their relative position in a market is probably more significant than the extent of concentration at a single point in time. (Gort, 1963, p. 51)

> The inability of large firms to maintain their market shares over a 'reasonably short' period could be persuasive evidence that these firms either had no monopoly power or that any power they might have had was only there for the short run. (Grossack, 1965, p. 302)

The 'instability index' devised by Hymer and Pashigian (1962) tracks changes in market shares over time:

$$I = \sum_{i=1}^{n} \left(\left| s_{it} - s_{i,t-1} \right| \right). \tag{1.1}$$

Since it is possible to have two industries with identical concentration ratios but very different instability indices, and since stability suggests the presence of collusion, the instability index captures an important aspect of competition. We use this index to analyse the results computed from the models developed in Chapters 2 and 3, below. Gort (1963) measures market share instability through statistical techniques which measure the degree of correlation of market shares over time (the extent to which shares at one point in time are dependent on those at another point). Others have used 'rank order' indices to measure the number of times that a 'switch' in market leadership occurred. If one believes that instability arises from industry- and technology-specific aspects of competition (that is, not simply from general 'animal spirits'), it is important for industrial policy makers to use such indices along with the more traditional concentration indices to gain insight into the competitive dynamics of industries.

3.3　Stochastic Firm-size Dynamics

The stochastic approach to firm-size dynamics arose mainly because of the dissatisfaction among industrial economists with static cost curve analysis which seemed incapable of explaining the role of technology- and firm-specific factors determining long-run market patterns (Chapter 3, below, is dedicated to this problem). The stochastic process most studied in this regard is *Gibrat's Law of Proportionate Growth*, which states that firm growth rates are independent identically distributed (iid) random variables independent of firm size (Gibrat,

1931; Kalecki, 1945; Ijiri and Simon, 1977). The size of a firm at time $t + 1$ is taken to be a function of its size at time t subject to random variation (Simon and Bonini, 1958; Geroski et al., 1997). Taking x_i to denote firm size, the size of firm i is governed by the following equation:

$$x_i(t) = \alpha + \beta_i x_i(t - 1) + \varepsilon_i(t) \qquad (1.2)$$

where $x_i(t)$ is the log size of firm i at time t, α is a growth component common to all firms, and ε is a random term. Gibrat's Law assumes that ε is iid and that for all $i, \beta_i = 1$ (that is, that the expected rate of growth is independent of the present size). The principal result in such models is that although firms might begin *ex ante* with equal growth prospects, differences in initial conditions and the presence of random events cause firms to soon diverge in size and market shares, causing a skewed size distribution (log normal) to emerge. The empirical evidence on Gibrat's Law is mixed, with some recent studies showing that firm growth rates and their variance tend to fall with size and age (Hall, 1987; Evans, 1987) and others which find evidence for the law by focussing on the large percentage of exits. Geroski and Machin (1993) find that Gibrat's Law is better suited to describe the growth process of relatively large firms. The main problem with this literature is that it makes market structure solely a result of random factors, which as is claimed by Geroski et al. (1997, p. 171): 'may be more an artifact of the models than of the data itself'.

A different use of stochastic concepts to study firm-size dynamics is found in the work of Arthur (1989, 1990) and David (1985, 1994). Arthur (1990) constructs a stochastic model of firm size in order to show how early events can strongly influence market outcomes when positive feedback is present. Using non-linear probability theory, in the form of a polya-urn process, he describes the interaction between a path-dependent process in which future size is pro-portional to current size and a stochastic process that introduces shocks. An orderly structure develops but the structure is 'selected' randomly: 'Small fortuitous events – unexpected orders, chance meetings with buyers, managerial whims – determine which [firms] achieve early sales and, over time, which firms dominate' (Arthur, 1994, p. 5). Although such studies have contributed greatly to our understanding of positive feedback and stochastic non-linear dynamics, here too there is little analysis regarding the *economic* mechanisms influencing firm size and differences between firms (that is intentionally not their focus).

A similar emphasis to that in Arthur and David, but from the perspective of an industrial economist, is found in Klepper and Graddy (1990) and Klepper (1996), where life-cycle dynamics under increasing returns to scale are studied. The combination of positive feedback and random events (randomly distributed innovative capabilities and timing of entry) causes the market structure to undergo an initial period of turbulence before reaching a concentrated state. Initial differences between firms created early on become magnified later due to the associated path-dependent dynamic (where size begets size), causing a concentrated market to develop:

> [C]hance events and exogenous factors that influence the number of potential entrants to the industry, the growth rate of incumbent firms, and the ease of imitation of the industry leaders will influence the ultimate number and size distribution of firms in the industry. (Klepper and Graddy, 1990, p. 27)

While it is unpredictable which firms will survive the shakeout, the mature phase is characterized by a stronger degree of predictability due to the cumulative forces:

> The result [of increasing returns] is a world in which initial firm differences get magnified as size begets size ... The starkness of the model precludes any departures from this evolutionary pattern. This can be remedied by allowing for random events that alter the relative standing of incumbents and potential entrants. If cohorts differ in terms of the distribution of their innovative expertise or if the innovative expertise of incumbents is undermined by certain types of technological changes, then later entrants may leapfrog over the industry leaders and the firms that eventually dominate the industry may not come from the earliest cohort of entrants. (Klepper, 1996, p. 581)

Having briefly described the difference between a static and a dynamic approach to market structure, we now focus on some of the empirical evidence supporting the latter. New insights regarding the stochastic approach are found in Chapter 3.

4 EMPIRICAL WORK ON FIRM SIZE AND INNOVATION

The relationship between firm size and innovation is a complex one due to the fact that both variables affect each other. Although many studies relating innovation to market structure are inspired by the writings of Joseph Schumpeter, sometimes they do not heed Schumpeter's own position that firm size is *endogenous* to the innovation process via 'creative destruction' (Kamien and Schwartz, 1982; Schumpeter, 1942). It is, in fact, the feedback embodied in this complex relationship which is responsible for the inconclusiveness of many econometric results on the topic.

The mechanism by which firm size affects innovation is tied to the relative advantages of large/small firms during the process of innovation. Reasons why large size can be advantageous for innovation include: capital market imperfections which give preference to large firms due to the stability of their internally generated funds; higher returns from R&D due to greater volume over which to spread costs (hence greater incentive to develop internal process improvements); high productivity of R&D due to the greater complementarities between manufacturing, marketing and financial planning; and the lower risk incurred from any one R&D project due to the more diversified portfolios of large firms. Both Schumpeter and Galbraith are known for their strong stances on this position:

> What we have got to accept is that [the large-scale establishment or unit of control] has come to be the most powerful engine of [economic] progress ... In this respect, perfect competition is not only impossible but inferior, and has no title to being set up as a model of ideal efficiency. (Schumpeter, 1942, p. 106)

Reasons why small firms may have advantages in innovation include: their greater managerial control and flexibility since research in large laboratories may become over-organized; their greater flexibility and motivation to foresee future changes in demand and technology; and their ability to attract scientists and entrepreneurs who are disillusioned by large bureaucratic firms. Schumpeter warned that the bureaucratization of inventive activity (to a certain extent more characteristic of large firms) could undermine capitalist development.

Empirical evidence suggests that there is no one answer to whether it is small or large firms which are more innovative; the relationship between firm size and innovation is sensitive to various factors such as the type of industry being considered, the underlying knowledge base of the technology, and the specific phase in the industry life-cycle. Thus, the appropriate question is not: ' "Which size firms have the relative advantage in innovation?", but rather "Under which circumstances do large or small firms have the relative innovative advantage?" ' (Acs and Audretsch, 1987, p. 573). Acs and Audretsch (1987) find that small firms tend to have a relative advantage in industries which are highly innovative, which use a large component of skilled labor, are low in R&D intensity, and which tend to be composed of a relatively high proportion of large firms. Other studies have also found that small firms have a relative advantage in innovation when innovation is radical as opposed to incremental, when the environment is characterized by strong uncertainty, and when production is more skill intensive rather than capital intensive. Uncertainty is especially high in situations of volatile changes in demand, prices and technological progress. Uncertainty is also high during the early stage of the industry life-cycle, when the product design has not yet been standardized and demand is unstable. In this phase, the flexibility of small new firms allows them to be the main sources of cost reduction and innovation (causing high rates of entry); while during the mature stage of the life-cycle, when the product and market demand have stabilized, economies of scale favoring large firms are strong and innovation becomes increasingly path-dependent, leading to a more stable oligopolistic structure. These findings seem to conform to some of the theoretical ideas by Abernathy and Wayne (1974) and Klein (1977), and to the empirical results by Abernathy and Utterback (1975), Acs and Audretsch (1987), Audretsch (1995) and Klepper (1996).

Ways in which the causation runs the other way around, that is, innovation affects firm size, is related to how innovation affects market structure. Innovation could be concentration-increasing if successful innovators rise to market dominance and can defend themselves successfully from imitators; or if vigorous innovation increases the variance of firms' growth rates under many versions of Gibrat's Law. Innovation can also affect market structure by increasing or decreasing the minimum efficient scale of production; if an innovation causes the minumum efficient scale of production (MES) to grow more rapidly than demand, then concentration will increase. This has been found to hold in electric power generation, chemical industries, cement, brewing, refrigerators, paints and batteries (Cohen and Levin, 1989).

The intensity (speed, vigor, opportunity) of innovation has been found to be an important factor in understanding the relationship between innovation and market structure. Geroski (1990) finds that vigorous innovative activity reduces concentration, and Mukhopadhyay (1985) has also found concentration to fall in high opportunity industries. Dosi (1984) finds that the semiconductor industry is more concentrated in countries that are not at the vanguard of technology. It has been found that product innovation, which is more radical (hence more vigorous) in nature than process innovation, tends to lead to a less concentrated market structure than process innovation. Lunn (1986) finds that while process innovation leads to higher concentration, product innovation leads to falling concentration (in the United States, three-quarters of R&D is dedicated to product innovation). Also, life-cycle studies find that entry rates are much higher than exit rates in the early stage of the life-cycle when product innovations are more important than process innovations (Klepper, 1996; Gort and Konakayama, 1982).

Scherer and Ross (1990) provide the following conclusion on the effect of innovation on firm size and market structure:

> The theory and evidence suggest a threshold concept of the most favorable climate for rapid technological change. A bit of monopoly power in the form of structural concentration is conducive to innovation, particularly when advances in the relevant knowledge base occur slowly. But very high concentration has a positive effect only in rare cases, and more often it is apt to retard progress by restricting the number of independent sources of initiative and by dampening firms' incentive to gain market position through accelerated R&D. Likewise, given the important role that technically audacious newcomers play in making radical innovations, it seems important that barriers to new entry be kept at modest levels. Schumpeter was right in asserting that perfect competition has no title to being established as the model of dynamic

efficiency ... yet neither do monopolies or cartels. ... What is needed for rapid technical progress is a subtle blend of competition and monopoly, with more emphasis on the former than the latter, and with the role of monopolistic elements diminishing when rich technological opportunities exist. (Scherer and Ross, 1990, p. 660)

5 SUMMARY

We began the chapter by placing the empirical regularities of firm size in the context of a theory of competition where the creation of differences between firms co-evolves with a selection mechanism. Two of the regularities addressed were the skewed size distribution of firms (variety in size) and periodic changes in market share instability, both observed across a wide range of industries and countries. To explore the origin and evolution of such patterns, we first reviewed static cost analysis, and finding this insufficient, we looked at more dynamic approaches. These included studies positing a stochastic relation between past and future size, which were criticized for providing little insight into the real economic mechanisms underlying change. The other dynamic approaches included studies positing a feedback relation between firm-specific character-istics and market structure. The life-cycle analysis was used as an example. To gain more insight into the dynamic relationship between firm size, innovation and market structure, Section 4 concentrated on a review of empirical studies regarding each link.

Although the empirical studies provided insight into the dynamic relation-ships, many of the results, regarding the relationship between firm size and innovation and the effect of innovation on market structure, were inconclu-sive. The inconclusiveness is due to (1) the importance of firm- and industry-specific variables, and (2) the fact that the non-linear interaction between these 'local' variables, prevents linear, or linearizing, econometric analysis from capturing the rich and complex nature of the underlying behavior. We saw, for example, that concentration can arise from innovation in industries where the knowledge base is tacit, where innovation is not vigorous, where technological opportunities are low and where imitation is difficult. Instead, in industries with high opportunity conditions, vigorous innovation, and more product than process innovation, innovation tends to reduce concentration (Dosi, 1984; Geroski, 1990; Lunn, 1986). We also saw that large firms are better innovators in capital-intensive industries, in advertising-intensive industries and in concentrated industries.

The limits to the static approach as well as the inconclusiveness of standard econometric techniques provided the motivation for exploring evolutionary dynamics in Section 3. An evolutionary framework of analysis is useful because mechanisms creating *differences* between firms are at the heart of both the empirical regularities regarding firm-size dynamics discussed in Section 3 and the innovation dynamics discussed in Section 4. We recall that one strength of evolutionary analysis is precisely the fact that differences between firms are not viewed as resulting from imperfections in the competitive mechanism but from the competitive dynamic itself. This allows the construction of a theory of competition which has at its center the emergence of inter-firm variety and the selection mechanisms which winnow in on the variety. The remainder of the chapter concentrates on the usefulness of methods in non-linear dynamics and computer simulation to construct an evolutionary model of industrial change. All three approaches have been found useful by social scientists interested in modeling the complexity discussed in Section 1.

6   DYNAMIC TECHNIQUES TO MODEL FIRM-SIZE DYNAMICS

Although there are various techniques in complex systems theory and non-linear dynamics which have been used to model evolutionary change, we focus here on three of these: (1) population dynamics via replicator equations; (2) critical fluctuations via master equations; and (3) state space exploration via computer simulation. Each is useful for exploring the emergence of macro patterns (order) from underlying (disequilibrium) micro dynamics. The models developed in Chapters 2 and 3 provide concrete examples of the usefulness of replicator equations and computer simulation techniques for exploring industry evolution.

6.1   Replicator Dynamics

The formalization of evolutionary theory has found one of its natural tools in the use of 'replicator dynamics'. Because of its focus on variety and 'novelty', evolutionary economic theory requires methodologies which can place variety at the center of analysis, rather than on the side line. The focus on variety and novelty requires full exploration of the state space, not *ex-ante* knowledge of it (as is instead necessary when the focus is on optimization). Replicator dynamics have been used to describe the population-based nature of evolutionary theories of selection, where the frequency of a species (technologies, firms, products and so on) grows differentially according to whether it has above- or below-average fitness, while average fitness itself varies in response to changes in the species' frequencies. Such growth processes have been labeled 'distance from *mean* dynamics' since what matters is not behavior of the mean (for example, representative agent) but *distance from mean behavior* (Metcalfe, 1994; Nelson, 1995).

Economic change described through replicator dynamics is different from change described through neoclassical theory. Since it is variety in agent characteristics which drives change, a world of 'representative agents' would imply no change. Furthermore, in replicator dynamics there is no reference to equilibrium positions or *states of rest* of any kind:

> Dynamic behavior is governed by replicator equations in which motions of relevant variables are related to comparisons between actual behavior and average behavior in the population. The variables may not approach an attractor but irrespective of this the mechanism generating their motions is clear. In this sense the replicator principle provides an important alternative basis for dynamics, a dynamic which exploits the variety in behavior in evolutionary systems. What we must not do is to confuse equilibrium qua state of rest with equilibrium qua pattern of coordinated behavior. Coordination is critical to any evolutionary argument but equilibrium in the sense of the absence of any internal tendency to change is not. (Metcalfe, 1994, p. 330)

The formalization of replicator dynamics is as follows (Schuster and Sigmund, 1983):

$$\dot{x}_i = Ax_i\left(E_i - \overline{E}\right), \ i = 1, \ n, \ \text{where } \overline{E} \equiv \sum x_i E_i, \tag{1.3}$$

where x_i represents the proportion of species i in a population of interacting species, that is, the relative frequency of the species i in the total population; E_i represents its 'reproductive fitness'; and $\overline{E}$ is the weighted average fitness level of the population. Respectively, these could represent the market share of a firm i, the cost of the firm, and the weighted average cost in the industry. The case originally investigated by Fisher (1930) was for constant E's where the system monotonically converges to a pure population consisting of the species with highest fitness. Others have focussed on the quadratic or cubic dependence of fitness on the frequency vector x (Hofbauer and Sigmund, 1988). The level of interactive complexity may be taken further by introducing additional dynamic variables and the lagged values of some of them.

Within this framework, agents with a variety of behavioral characteristics coexist and define a joint population distribution defined by its statistical moments (mean, variance, skewness). The statistical moments of the population distribution continually change via the selection process, where the rate of change of the moments of one order is a function of the moments of a higher order (Metcalfe, 1994). One of the statistical properties of replicator dynamics is Fisher's Fundamental Theorem (Fisher, 1930), which states that the rate of change of mean fitness is proportional to the variance (weighted by the share) of fitness characteristics in the population:

$$\frac{d}{dt}\left(\overline{E}_x\right) = -fV_x\left(E_i\right). \tag{1.4}$$

The fundamental theorem is part of a more general principle, 'Fisher's Principle', which states that patterns of change are dependent on patterns of differential behavior (the theorem is a particular case of the principle when change is necessarily *progressive*). Metcalfe states:

> In essence, the Fisher principle rationalizes a dynamics of discovery, the unfolding of economic structures as a consequence of variety in behavior. In terms of economic methodology, Fisher's principle sets the agenda for evolutionary economics where the focus is on: 'the meaning of variety in a given context; the appropriate measurement of variety; and the relation of measured variety to change at the population level'. (Metcalfe, 1994, p. 330)

Silverberg (1983, 1987), Silverberg et al. (1988), Metcalfe (1994), and Mazzucato (1998) use replicator dynamics to study the dynamic structure governing firm size and efficiency in an industry driven by Schumpeterian competition. For example, Silverberg et al. (1988) use a replicator equation to study market share dynamics which emerge from diffusion processes in evolutionary environments characterized by technological and behavioral diversity among the economic agents. They define firm fitness as a weighted sum of its unit costs and its delivery delay.

6.2 Master Equations

Whereas replicator dynamics have a foundation in biology, dynamics based on 'master equations' have a foundation in physics. The general approach under which the master-equation analysis falls, is referred to as the *self-organization* paradigm. The main goal of the self-organization approach, introduced to the social sciences by Haken (1978), who labeled the paradigm as 'synergetics', is to derive the properties of multi-component systems on the macroscopic level from their constituent components on the elementary microscopic level. Weidlich and Haag, define 'synergetics' as the 'science of collective static or dynamic phenomena in closed or open multicomponent systems with "cooperative" interaction occurring between the units of the system' (Weidlich and Haag, 1982, p. 15).

The foundation of the self-organization approach is composed of non-linear dynamics, systems theory and statistical physics. In physics (and as will be argued, in economics), there are complex interactions at the *micro level*, such as the interactions between molecules of a gas, which may be characterized by specific parameters like their position and momentum vectors. The *macroscopic level* is characterized by a few collective macroscopic observable quantities, called 'gross variables' or macro variables, such as pressure, density, entropy, correlation functions and other parameters characterizing the macroscopic state or dynamic space–time structure of fields and particles.

The economy can be viewed as a multi-component system composed of 'units', such as customers, firms, industries and techniques. The system is open because there exists an internal interaction between the units and an interaction with the external environment. Each unit exists in one of several different possible states. If the external conditions of an open system are changed by varying certain control parameters, the system may undergo a radical change in its macroscopic global state if the control parameters pass certain critical values. Such transitions are denoted as 'phase transitions'.

Part of the problem is to explain which macro variables may be relevant under given circumstances and to describe their dynamics by appropriate equations of motion. Phenomenological derivations of such equations are possible by making assumptions and approximations about the system in question. Exact equations of motion for macro variables contain the interactions between the macro variables as well as the rapidly fluctuating random forces due to the influence of micro variables.

The analogy between the physico-chemical system and an economic system (for example, composed of changing firm sizes, techniques or profit rates) is due not to the analogy between the units but rather to the general probabilistic laws governing the statistical dynamics of multi-component systems. In transitions from the micro-level units of analysis, to the macro-level units, the concept of 'economic configuration' is useful. The economic configuration could describe the distribution of firm sizes over the sub-population of firms, considered as an appropriate set of macro variables for the economy. The dynamics of interacting populations then consists of a theory concerning the structural development of this economic configuration, or of quantities derived from it, with time. This is similar to evolutionary methodology outlined in the quotation by Dosi (1984), already cited above:

> The patterns of evolution of the system are determined by the interaction between structural constraints ... and behavioral degrees of freedom of each economic agent. ... We shall be essentially concerned with the evolution of the structural boundaries of these degrees of behavioral freedom. (Dosi, 1984, p. 11)

In physics a probabilistic description of the motion of macro variables proves to be adequate even when the details of the micro fluctuations of the system are unknown. Thus master equations can be used to model phenomena like technological diffusion via 'transition probabilities', which describe the likelihood that a firm will switch from one technique to another.

If the control parameters governing the dynamic behavior of the system (described by the master equations) attain certain critical values due to internal or external interactions, the macro variables may move into a critical area out of which highly divergent alternative paths are possible. In this situation, small unpredictable micro fluctuations may decide into which of the diverging paths the behavior of the economy will bifurcate. This last aspect is similar to the type of dynamics described by Arthur (1990), David (1985) and Klepper and Graddy (1990), mentioned in Section 3, above, on the effect of initial random events on industrial dynamics characterized by increasing returns to scale.

Examples in economic literature which have used master equations to analyse the emergence and evolution of macroscopic structures from the underlying microdiversity include Silverberg (1988) and Weidlich and Braun (1992).

6.2   Computer Simulation

Computer simulation techniques are useful for studying industrial dynamics because non-linear behavior is best studied through modeling techniques which do not constrain the degree of feedback among the variables. Section 4 described the non-linear relationship embodied in the process by which costs affect market shares, which in turn affect costs, together determining the path of industrial evolution. This differs from the one-way (linear) causation specified in the structure–conduct–performance approach which motivated much econometric work in industrial organization. Although recent work has emphasized the feedback loops between structure, conduct and performance (Jacquemin, 1987), to allow the underlying non-linearity to really play itself out, dynamic non-linear techniques must also be used. This is because feedback causes complexity to be introduced into models, which can only be explored with techniques which do not put constraints on the degree of non-linearity:

> Feedback exists whenever decisions made by agents in a system alter the state of the system, thereby giving rise to new information that conditions future decisions. The dynamics of a system emerge out of the interaction of the multiple feedback loops in its structure. Feedback loops may be self-reinforcing (positive feedback) or self-correcting (negative feedback) . ... The interaction of multiple feedback processes in complex nonlinear systems often causes disequilibria to persist. ... Nonlinearities contribute significantly to a system's evolutionary behavior because they cause the strength of its feedback loops, and hence its 'active structure,' to change over time. ... The nonlinearities in dynamic systems mean the active structure or dominant feedback loops can change endogenously, and as a result possess multiple equilibria. (Radzicki and Sterman, 1994, p. 68)

When there is feedback between variables, the emergent behavior is often too complex to be solved by closed-form mathematical solutions. Furthermore, the dynamics which emerge for the case of many firms is often qualitatively very different (more subtle and rich in structure) from the case of two firms.

Simulation analysis allows evolutionary systems, characterized by a large number of possible trajectories, to be explored creatively. The exploration is useful if taken in steps; for example, first distinguishing deterministic from stochastic dynamics, and then altering one parameter at a time since non-intuitive results may emerge with small changes in one parameter even in purely deterministic dynamics. Systems characterized by path-dependency, described in Section 3, above, are particularly vulnerable to non-linear, sometimes chaotic, behavior in which small changes in initial conditions produce lasting and irreversible effects (Arthur, 1989; David, 1994). Although it is the 'complexity' of evolutionary systems which makes simulation techniques useful, it is this author's experience that simulation analysis is most useful for exploring 'simple' complex models, that is models with few parameters and in which the simulation results are traceable to the variation in specific parameters. Simulation methodology is less useful in models that attempt to take many factors into consideration, since this increases the factor of complexity to such a degree, that 'anything can happen'. The latter case, along with cases in which simulation is used when analytical solutions could be derived, have caused some economists to be justifiably suspicious of simulation methodology. That same suspicion in simple simulation models in which complex evolutionary dynamics make analytical solutions impossible is less justifiable since it stems more from general non-acceptance of models which do not contain optimization and closed-form analytical solutions. As argued here and elsewhere, neither optimization analysis nor closed-form analytical solutions are suitable for exploring processes which endogenously create novelty and which are (thus) inherently unpredictable (Foley, 1997).

Silverberg et al. (1988), Dosi et al. (1995) and Mazzucato (1998) use simulation methodology to explore the implications of different Schumpeterian scenarios concerning innovation, firm size and market structure. Dosi et al. (1995) build a model which attempts to explain empirical regularities in firm-size distributions, firm growth patterns, and market instability as emergent properties deriving from non-equilibrium interactions among technologically heterogeneous firms. They use simulation techniques to explore the implications of different types of technological learning (technological regimes) and market interactions (market regimes). The exercises show that intersectoral variety in the observed industrial structures and dynamics can be interpreted on the grounds of these underlying technological and market factors. The feedback between the learning regimes and the market structure would be very hard to explore fully without the use of simulation techniques.

The next two chapters provide concrete examples of how *distance from mean dynamics* and computer simulation techniques can be used for exploring the market structure patterns that emerge from the interaction between firm size and innovation.

2. A computational model of economies of scale and market share instability: a deterministic analysis[*]

1 INTRODUCTION

This chapter uses computer simulation techniques to study the origin and evolution of market concentration and market share instability during the industry life-cycle. A reduced-form evolutionary model is used to generate a typology of market structures from different assumptions regarding the effect of firm size on the rate of cost reduction (innovation). The typology of market structures which emerges from the simulations is compared to theoretical and empirical studies which have found concentration and instability to be tied to industry-specific variables: instability is higher in the early phase of the industry life-cycle, in industries characterized by radical innovation, and in industries where innovation is undertaken mainly by small firms (Acs and Audretsch, 1990; Klein, 1977; Klepper, 1996).

Whereas most studies on firm size and costs focus on the effect of firm size on the direction of costs (static returns to scale), here the focus is on the effect of firm size on the *rate of cost reduction* (dynamic returns to scale). Analytical results for the latter case, referred to here as 'static' economies of scale, are well known: unique equilibria of market shares in the case of decreasing returns to scale or *negative feedback*, and multiple equilibria in the case of increasing returns to scale or *positive feedback* (Arthur et al., 1987; Arthur, 1989; David, 1985, 1994). This has caused economists, critical of traditional equilibrium analysis, to consider negative feedback processes uninteresting and to focus attention on the economic implications of positive feedback (Krugman, 1979; Metcalfe, 1994).

In contrast, the current study not only does not ignore negative feedback, but also finds a particular kind of negative feedback to be very illuminating for economists interested in disequilibrium dynamics. This negative feedback is that embodied in the relationship between size and innovation: when an increase in firm size causes the firm's rate of cost reduction to fall. In exploring the effect of size on the rate of cost reduction, that is, *dynamic* economies of scale, the simulation model finds that both positive and negative feedback produce multiple equilibria, but that only negative feedback produces the instability in market shares similar to that found in empirical studies linking market share changes to industry-specific variables.

The modeling framework is an evolutionary one with focus on the co-evolution of variety between firm characteristics and a selection mechanism winnowing in on the variety. While selection allows only the fittest firms to grow, inter-firm variety is generated from differences in the ability of small and large firms to innovate and from the interaction of these differences with initial conditions. As discussed in Chapter 1, replicator equations are especially useful for such a model because of their emphasis on 'distance from mean' dynamics, which allows firm evolution to be viewed not through the representative agent but through the degree to which agents differ from the representative agent; in a world of average behavior there is *no change* (Hofbauer and Sigmund, 1988; Metcalfe, 1994).

Computer simulation techniques are used for the reasons outlined at the end of Chapter 1: non-linear behavior is best studied through modeling techniques which do not constrain the degree of feedback among the variables. The non-linearity here refers to the possibility that costs affect market shares, which in turn affect costs, together determining the path of industrial evolution; market structure is *endogenous* to the process of innovation. This differs from the one-way causation specified in traditional industrial organization theory between the structure of the market, the conduct of firms and firm performance (Jacquemin, 1987).

The goal of the simulations is to catalogue the different types of market share patterns which emerge from variations in empirically relevant parameters, and then to compare these patterns to empirical regularities in industrial dynamics. The two principal regularities of interest are the skewed size distribution of firms and periodic market share instability. The parameters include the variance of the initial distribution of costs (that is, the degree to which firms' fitness characteristics differ from one another when they begin competing), the industry-specific average speed of cost reduction (dependent on the speed of diffusion in the industry, the tacitness of the knowledge base and so on), the time period in the industry life-cycle in which a change in feedback regime occurs, and of course the functional form of the cost equation which describes the type of dynamic returns to scale being investigated.

While the reduced-form nature of the model implies that it cannot capture the specificities of one particular industry or firm, its purpose is to capture general properties of a wide group of industries which are not easily revealed in detailed models. Understanding such general properties 'clears the ground' for more specific assumptions to be explored regarding demand, entry, price and so on. The abstraction from details allows the analysis to focus on the relatively unexplored disequilibrium dynamics which emerge from negative feedback, and to posit a clear difference between firm- and industry-specific factors which affect market structure. One element that is purposely omitted is the effect of stochastic shocks

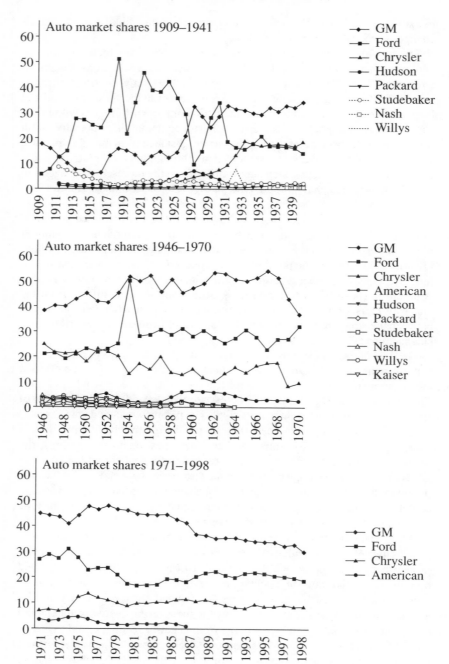

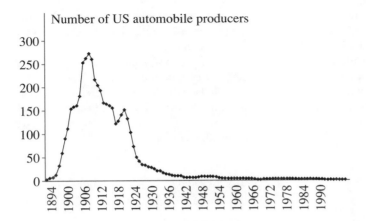

Sources: Number of firms taken from *Ward's Automotive Yearbook* (1936–95), Ward's Communications, Detroit. Market shares 1911–37: Federal Trade Commission (1939), US Dept of Congress Manuscript (pp. 29, 682–3, 715, 749–50, 812); 1940–95: *Ward's Automotive Yearbook* (1936–95).

Figure 2.1   Market shares of US automobile producers and number of firms

on market structure. Such shocks are fundamental to capture the idiosyncratic aspects of innovation and the role of early 'small' events. Yet in order to uncover the non-intuitive properties of the deterministic dynamics, the treatment of randomness is left to Chapter 3 where the focus lies solely on the effect of shocks on the relationship between firm size, market structure and innovation.

2   EMPIRICAL REGULARITIES AND THE MEASUREMENT OF COMPETITION

The study is motivated by two regularities widely documented in industrial dynamics: (1) the 'skewed-size distribution' of firms found to exist across industries (Hart and Prais, 1956; Simon and Bonini, 1958; Ijiri and Simon, 1977), and (2) the alternating periods of market share instability during an industry's life-cycle (Gort, 1963; Hymer and Pashigan, 1962; Klein, 1977). Figure 2.1 illustrates that in the US auto industry there has been a prevalence of market concentration, with changing firm numbers, accompanied by alternating periods of market share (in)stability. Although the level of concentration is the focus of most studies on competition, it is evident here that it is more the level of instability which varies over time. Some periods, such as 1909–41, were characterized by market share instability, while others, such as

1971–98, were characterized by more stability in market shares and more concentration. The large change in the number of firms, which characterized the
entire period, is seen clearly in the fourth graph.

Figure 2.1 illustrates the inadequacy of using (only) traditional concentration
indices to measure competition; there are certain phases of the history of the
automobile industry (for example, 1909–41) which are characterized by both
a high degree of concentration (indicating the *lack* of competition) and a high
degree of instability (indicating the *presence* of competition). Figure 2.2 uses
an instability index (defined already in Chapter 1 as

$$I = \sum_{i=1}^{n} \left(s_{it} - s_{i,t-1} \right)$$

where s_{it} is the market share of firm i at time t and n is the number of firms) to
trace the evolution of market share instability over time and compares this to
the change in concentration measured through the Herfindahl index

$$\left(H = \sum_{i=1}^{n} s_i^2 \right).$$

The figure illustrates increasing concentration and varying levels of instability,
with a generally higher level of instability in the beginning of the life-cycle.

Similar patterns have been found in other industries such as aircraft (Phillips,
1971; Klein, 1977), television sets (Datta, 1971), semi-conductors (Malerba,
1985; Gruber, 1994), and tires (French, 1991). These patterns suggest that there
are persistent economic factors generating industry concentration and periodic
market share stability.

Studies seeking to explain these regularities have tended to separate the
analysis of concentration from that of instability rather than viewing them as
outcomes of a common underlying dynamic.[1] Explanations regarding the cause
of concentration have focussed on two main processes: (1) the optimal allocation
of scarce factors of production, and/or (2) the random nature of firm growth
patterns. The stochastic approach arose principally due to the dissatisfaction
among industrial economists with static cost curve analysis which is incapable
of explaining the role of technology- and firm-specific factors determining
long-run patterns (Kaldor, 1985). This approach typically assumes the size of
a firm at time $t + 1$ to be a function of its size at time t subject to random
variation. The stochastic process most studied in this regard is Gibrat's Law of
Proportionate Growth, which states that firm growth rates are iid random
variables independent of firm size (Gibrat, 1931; Ijiri and Simon, 1977; Kalecki,
1945; Simon and Bonini, 1958). The principal result in such models is that

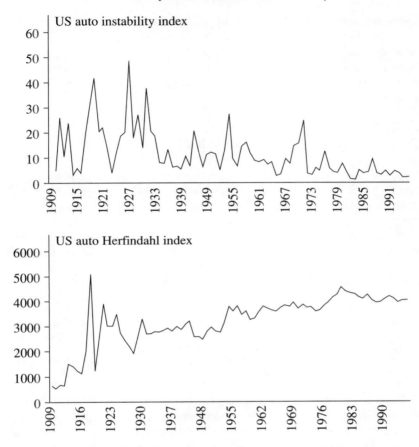

Figure 2.2 Instability and concentration in the US automobile industry

although firms begin *ex ante* with equal growth prospects, random events soon cause firms to diverge in size and a skewed size distribution to emerge (lognormal). A problem with the stochastic approach is that it makes market structure solely a result of random factors. The reliance on randomness ignores empirical case studies which refer to specific economic mechanisms, concerning firm size and innovation, which might generate such patterns (Audretsch, 1995; Klepper, 1996).

This chapter takes an alternative approach to modeling market share dynamics. It emphasizes the interaction between industry- and firm-specific variables. The former includes the ease of innovation in the industry (defined as 'technological opportunity') and the latter includes firm size and initial firm efficiency. The structural dynamic described in the cost curves is motivated by the Schumpeterian literature on the feedback between innovation, firm size and market structure and the life-cycle literature which looks at how these relations change over time (Abernathy and Utterback, 1975; Audretsch, 1995; Kamien and Schwartz, 1975; Klepper, 1996).[2] Simulation techniques are used to study the degree of market share instability and concentration which emerge from different parameter configurations.

3   FIRM SIZE AND INNOVATION

The common usage of the term (dis)economies of scale, referred to here as 'static' (dis)economies of scale, refers to the (rise) fall in unit costs which arises from an increase in quantity produced. Diseconomies of scale pose a limit to the size of the firm by punishing large size with rising unit costs. It is this aspect of the traditional U-shaped long-run average cost curve that allows market structure to be predicted easily. Brian Arthur, whose well-known studies focus on positive feedback in order to avoid the unique equilibria associated with negative feedback, describes the latter as follows:

> An example is the competition between water and coal to generate electricity. As hydroelectric plants take more of the market, engineers must exploit more costly dam sites, thereby increasing the chance that coal-fired plant will be cheaper. As coal plants take more of the market, they bid up the price of coal ... and so tip the balance toward hydropower. The two technologies end up sharing the market in a predictable proportion. (Arthur, 1994, p. 2)

The presence of static increasing returns to scale allows the firm that captures an early advantage to *remain* the leader and hence the asymptotic market structure to be determined by early (random) events and the system to be characterized by multiple equilibria and 'lock-in' (Arthur, 1990; David, 1985):

> Diminishing returns imply a single equilibrium point for the economy, but positive feedback – increasing returns – makes for many equilibrium points. There is no guarantee that the particular economic outcome selected from among the many alternatives will be the 'best' one ... Once random events select a particular path, the choice may become locked in regardless of the advantages of the alternatives ... Predictable and shared markets are no longer guaranteed. (Arthur, 1994, p. 1)

Metcalfe's (1994) use of replicator dynamics to model internal and external economies of scale concentrates on the analytical results for such static (dis)economies of scale. Both Metcalfe and Arthur are economists whose interest in disequilibrium and non-linear dynamics led them to study positive feedback mechanisms.

It is argued below that static economies of scale are not adequate for understanding the dynamics of firm size and innovation for several reasons. First, the term 'negative feedback' has been wrongly associated with only predictable and unique equilibria. While this is true for *static* diseconomies of scale, it is not true for *dynamic* diseconomies of scale. The chapter illustrates that the latter is able to generate multiple equilibria and instability in market shares. Second, it will be argued that the dynamics of innovation are not adequately captured through the static conception of economies of scale. An alternative description, more consistent with case studies on firm growth and innovation, is the conception of dynamic economies of scale; the effect of firm size on the rate of cost reduction. Since firms' rate of cost reduction is directly related to their innovation activities, the subject brings us to the long-standing debate on whether small or large firms are more innovative. Schumpeter himself had different positions on this matter, emphasizing in *The Theory of Economic Development* (1934) the important role of flexible and entrepreneurial firms in the innovation process, and in *Capitalism, Socialism and Democracy* (1942) the role of large firms in financing expensive R&D activities.[3] Some economists, such as Galbraith (1952) and Kamien and Schwartz (1975), have tended to follow Schumpeter's second position claiming that since profit-maximizing firms will only innovate if they can capture a temporary rent from innovation, it is large firms with strong market power and the necessary capital to pay for expensive R&D which will have advantages in innovation. Others, such as Schumacher (1973), have instead placed more emphasis on Schumpeter's early position.

As reviewed in Chapter 1, empirical evidence suggests that there is no one answer to whether small or large firms are more innovative; the relationship between firm size and innovation is sensitive to various factors such as the type of industry being considered, the underlying knowledge base of the technology, and the specific phase in the industry life-cycle. Thus, the appropriate question is not: ' "Which size firms have the relative advantage in innovation", but rather "Under which circumstances do large or small firms have the relative innovative advantage?" ' (Acs and Audretsch, 1987, 573).

Acs and Audretsch (1987) find that small firms tend to have a relative advantage in industries which are highly innovative, which use a large component of skilled labor, are low in R&D intensity, and which tend to be composed of a relatively high proportion of large firms. Other studies have also found that small firms have a relative advantage in innovation when innovation is radical as opposed to incremental, when the environment is characterized by strong uncertainty, and when production is more skill intensive rather than capital intensive (Abernathy and Wayne, 1974; Klein, 1977; Jovanovic and MacDonald, 1994a; Klepper, 1996). Uncertainty is especially high in situations of volatile changes in demand, prices and technological progress. In such situations, and in the absence of significant barriers to entry, small firms may enter the industry with their more novel and responsive ideas, products and processes, challenging established firms and continuously disrupting the current way of production, organization and distribution, and wiping away the quasi-rents associated with earlier innovations. The advantage of small firms is tied to the idea that firms with large market shares may become too 'lethargic' to adapt well to uncertainty, being more concerned with maintaining the status quo than with initiating novel cost-reduction techniques: '[T]he highly specialized production process lacked the balance to handle the new product ... management needs to recognize that conditions stimulating innovation are different from those favoring efficient, high-volume, established operations' (Abernathy and Wayne, 1974, pp. 116, 118).

Large firms have instead been found to have an advantage in innovation in industries which are capital intensive, concentrated, and which produce a differentiated good (Acs and Audretsch, 1987).[4] They also tend to have advantages in stable environments where tastes do not change quickly and where the product is standardized. Under these circumstances, economies of specialization generate cumulative advantages for existing leaders, allowing large firms to accumulate retained earnings which can be used to finance increasingly expensive R&D, and to hire more skilled managers and engineers. Large firms with more assets than small firms have in fact been proven to receive more favorable interest rates and loans to raise capital than smaller firms (Blitz et al., 1987). Thus a cumulative pattern emerges where large firms are able to reduce their costs faster on a given set of techniques as well as to finance and search for new cost-reducing techniques. These advantages can become 'barriers to entry' for small firms. Leaders remain leaders; initial advantages become permanent (absolute) advantages.

Another factor, and the one most stressed in the model below, on which the relationship between firm size and innovation depends, is the specific time period in an industry's history. The industry 'life-cycle' refers to the competitive situation of firms in the early, intermediate and mature stages of an industry's evolution. The general argument is that during the early stage of an industry's history, when the product and market are uncertain, and the knowledge base is still generic, the flexibility of small new firms allows them to be the main sources of cost reduction and innovation (causing high rates of entry); while during the mature stage of the life-cycle, when the product and market demand have stabilized, economies of scale favoring large firms are strong and innovation becomes increasingly path-dependent, leading to a more stable oligopolistic structure. This hypothesis seems to conform well to the results of many empirical studies (Abernathy and Utterback, 1975; Acs and Audretsch, 1987; Audretsch, 1995; Klepper, 1996). Hence as regards instability and concentration, one would expect the early stage of the life-cycle to be characterized by unstable market shares and the mature stage by market share stability and concentration. Some versions of the life-cycle argument emphasize the continuous alternation between the above phases as new innovations cause industrial routines to be periodically uprooted (Malerba and Orsenigo, 1996).

Rothwell and Dodgson (1996) summarize the advantages of large firms as 'material' and those of small firms as 'behavioral'. Klein (1977) frames the argument in terms of periods of 'static efficiency' in which large firms have a relative advantage (exploitation of the existing production possibility frontier) versus periods of 'dynamic efficiency' in which small firms have a relative advantage (extension of the frontier). Others still have referred to the former as advantages to 'exploitation' and the latter as advantages to 'exploration' (March, 1991). We expand on this further in Chapter 3.

Having developed the economic intuition behind the relation between firm size and innovation, we now use it to guide our modeling procedure.

4   THE MODEL

In what follows, a simulation model is built which uses insights regarding *dynamic* (dis)economies of scale to study the origin and evolution of market concentration and market share instability. We model the time-path of firm market shares through a replicator equation and the time-path of unit costs through a series of 'nested' equations which depict *dynamic* increasing and decreasing returns to scale. We assume an industry composed of n firms, each characterized by a market share s_i and a unit cost c_i. Although firms are assumed here to have exited when their market shares are very low, no new firms 'enter'. Equation (2.1) states that a firm's market share grows if the firm is characterized by below-average unit costs (that is, above-average fitness) and falls if it is characterized by above-average unit costs:

$$\dot{s}_i = \lambda \cdot s_i(\bar{c} - c_i), \quad i = 1, \ ..., \ n \tag{2.1}$$

$$\bar{c} \equiv \sum_i c_i s_i \ = \ \text{weighted average cost, where} \ \sum_i s_i = 1. \tag{2.1a}$$

The average cost is an average weighted by shares. The parameter λ determines the speed of selection: the speed at which firm market shares react to differences between firm efficiency characteristics. The speed of selection could be made a firm- or an industry-specific parameter, which either remains constant or evolves over time. As an industry-specific parameter, a high λ would describe an industry with a strong competitive adjustment mechanism which might evolve endogenously with the changing Herfindahl index (as a result of selection). Although we assume that the speed of selection λ is always equal to 1, we comment briefly on the effect of changing its value after the simulation of simple selection below. Geroski and Mazzucato (1999) focus on the role of consumer price sensitivity in determining the speed of selection.

Equation (2.2) illustrates 'Fisher's principle' (Fisher, 1930) which is derived from equations (2.1) and (2.1a). The theorem states that the rate of change of mean fitness is a function of the degree of variety in fitness levels across the population; the more variety exists among firm costs, the greater is the absolute change in the weighted average cost. Once variety disappears, the average cost remains constant.

$$d\bar{c}/dt = \sum_i c_i s_i(\bar{c} - c_i) = \bar{c}^2 - \sum_i s_i c_i^2 = \sum_i s_i \bar{c}^2 - \sum_i s_i \bar{c}_i^2 = \sum_i s_i(\bar{c}^2 - c_i^2) = -\mathrm{Var}(c_i).$$

(2.2)

When selection occurs among *constant* fitness characteristics, Fisher's principle becomes the 'fundamental theorem of natural selection' which adds a progressive element to the direction of change; the rate of *improvement* of mean behavior (rate of reduction of average cost) is proportional to the variance in population fitness. In the one-dimensional case of constant costs, the direction of change is determinate; selection leads to higher average fitness (Metcalfe, 1994).

4.1   Static Economies of Scale

The advantage of using equation. (2.1) to depict the evolution of market shares is that its analytical solution(s) allows us to study the dynamics of economies of scale without (for the moment) including a separate equation for costs. We illustrate this below for the case of a duopoly where s_1 refers to the market share of firm 1. The time-path of firm 1's market share is derived by substituting the average cost equation (2.1a) into equation (2.1) above:

$$\dot{s}_1 = \lambda s_1(s_1 c_1 + s_2 c_2 - c_1)$$

$$\dot{s} = \lambda s_1(1 - s_1)(c_2 - c_1).$$

(2.3)

Equation (2.3) allows us to study economies of scale by exploring different assumptions on the last term $(c_2 - c_1)$. We consider three possible cases:

$(c_2 - c_1) = \text{constant}$ constant returns to scale   (2.3a)
$(c_2 - c_1) = g(s_2 - s_1);$ $g'(x) > 0$, decreasing returns to scale   (2.3b)
$(c_2 - c_1) = f(s_2 - s_1);$ $f'(x) < 0$, increasing returns to scale   (2.3c)

In the following we let $g(x) = x$ and $f(x) = -x$. We use the above three cases (2.3a–c) to explore the feedback mechanisms between market shares and unit costs embodied in the concept of static increasing and decreasing returns to scale.

Simple selection

Case (2.3a) assumes that as the market share of firm 1 increases, the relative cost dis/advantage of firm 1 remains the same. In the evolutionary literature when agents' fitness characteristics remain constant, the system is referred to as 'simple selection'; selection occurs over a set of constant fitness characteristics (Hofbauer and Sigmund, 1988). The equilibrium solution of this constant cost scenario is intuitive: the firm with the lowest cost will capture the entire market in the long run. We first illustrate this equilibrium solution analytically and then via computer simulation. With constant costs, the analytical solution to equation (2.1) is equation (2.4) below:

$$ds_1/dt = \beta s_1(1 - s_1), \quad \text{where} \quad \beta = \lambda s(\overline{c_2 - c_1})$$

$$\frac{ds_1}{s_1(1 - s_1)} = \beta dt \Rightarrow \int_0^t \frac{ds_1}{s_1(1 - s_1)} = \beta(t), \quad \text{and solving for } s(t):$$

$$s_1(t) = \left[1 + \frac{1 - s_1(0)}{s_1(0)} e^{-\beta t}\right]^{-1} \quad \text{(see Appendix for proof)}. \tag{2.4}$$

Equation (2.4) allows us to predict the equilibrium market shares of the two firms solely through our knowledge of their (relative) initial costs: as $t \to \infty$, if β is positive (that is, if $c_2 > c_1$), then firm 1 captures the entire market, otherwise its market share goes to 0 (similarly for firm 2):

$$\text{if } \frac{c_2(0)}{c_1(0)} > 1, \text{ then } s_1(t) \to 1$$

$$\text{if } \frac{c_2(0)}{c_1(0)} < 1, \text{ then } s_1(t) \to 0.$$

Thus in the case of constant costs, there is a stable long-run equilibrium of market shares: whichever firm has a cost advantage at $t = 0$, will in the limit obtain a market share equal to 1. This equilibrium is independent of initial conditions; any combination of initial costs will lead to systematic divergence of the two firms' positions. The only way that both firms can co-exist is if they begin with the same costs, but then there is no evolution of market shares!

Below we illustrate the same result through the use of computer simulation. The initial conditions are that market shares begin *equally* distributed between the *n* firms ($s_i = 1/n$) and costs begin randomly distributed (normally distributed between 0 and 1). Although costs do not change, the 'progressive' element of selection in equation (2.1) causes the (weighted) average industry cost to fall. We see in Figure 2.3 that the firm with the lowest initial cost captures the entire market.

A full set of results, using the statistics developed above, are illustrated for the case of *n* = 10 firms in Figure 2.4.

With constant costs the emergent market structure is predictable; the powerful force of selection causes the firm with the lowest initial cost to

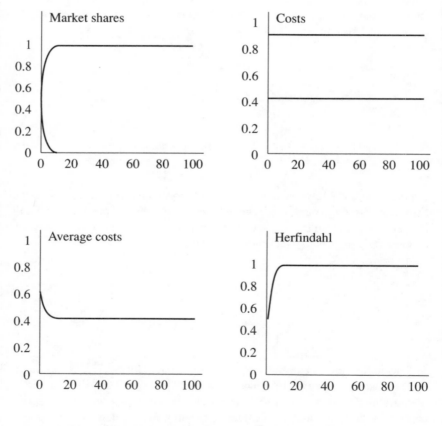

Figure 2.3   Simple selection: equation (2.1) for n = 2 *firms with* constant costs

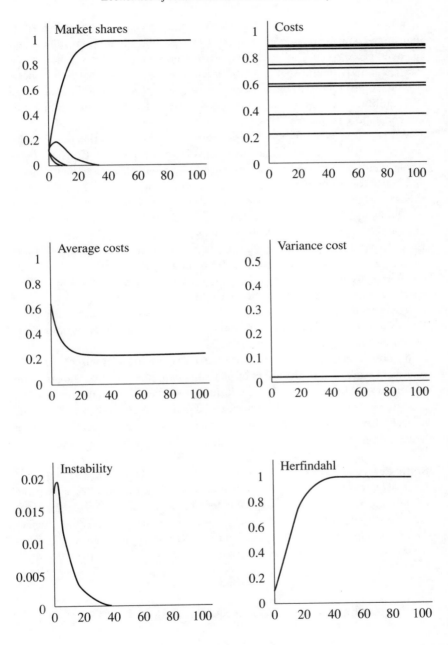

Figure 2.4   Simple selection: equation (2.1) for n = 10 *firms with* constant *costs*

dominate the entire market.[5] The Herfindahl index reaches the value of 1, indicating complete monopoly. Market shares reach an equilibrium value when the average cost is no longer different from the surviving firms' costs: when $c_i = \bar{c}$, $\dot{s}_i = 0$. Different speed of adjustment coefficients (λ) change the speed at which convergence to the monopoly structure is reached but do not change the equilibrium solution itself: the higher value of λ, the faster the market converges to a monopoly solution.

With constant costs, although variety drives selection, selection destroys the variety so that selection dominates the evolutionary process. Constant costs are an example of strong 'inertia': inertia allows initial leaders to remain leaders and hence for strong path-dependency to occur. Below we shall see that even if costs are changing, inertia embodied in very slow innovation also causes a monopoly to emerge *independently* of the underlying process causing costs to change. The case of simple selection is not very interesting since it assumes that firms do not actively seek to reduce costs (to *change* their competitive fitness strategically). The empirical work of 'new industrial organization' theory has countered this assumption by emphasizing (and documenting) the role of firm-specific actions in *altering* industry market structure through active cost-reduction strategies. The non-linear relation between market structure, firm conduct and economic performance is not compatible with the simple selection framework (Jacquemin, 1987).

We now drop the assumption of constant costs and consider the case of static returns to scale, that is, the effect of increases in market share on the direction of unit costs. After deriving the equilibrium properties of static returns to scale, the core of the chapter analyses the case of dynamic returns to scale, that is, the effect of market share on the rate of cost reduction, which is in fact more relevant in a Schumpeterian world where firms compete through strategic innovation.

Static decreasing returns

Decreasing returns to scale implies that an increase in firm size has a negative effect on firm efficiency (fitness). We depict this phenomenon (case 2.3b) for a duopoly by substituting $(c_2 - c_1) = g\,(s_2 - s_1)$ into equation (2.3) above, where the function $g\,(g'\,(x) > 0)$ illustrates that as s_1 increases, c_1 increases (an increase in firm size reduces firm fitness). Assuming $g\,(x) = x$, we may write this as:

$$c_2 - c_1 = s_2 - s_1 = (1 - s_1) - s_1 = 1 - 2s_1$$

which transforms equation (2.3) into equation (2.5):

$$\dot{s}_1 = \lambda s_1 (1 - s_1)(1 - 2s_1). \tag{2.5}$$

Figure 2.5 depicts the phase diagram for equation (2.5). The arrows illustrate that decreasing returns to scale lead to a unique and stable market equilibrium: for *any* initial distribution of market shares, the shares will converge to a uniform value (= $1/n$). The equilibrium point is stable since a perturbation in either direction will cause market shares to come back to that equilibrium point.

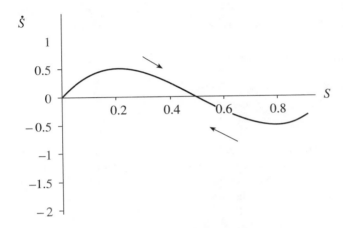

Figure 2.5   Static decreasing returns to scale

This is the standard result found in neoclassical microeconomic theory; diminishing returns to scale create negative feedback mechanisms which limit the size of a firm. It is the U-shaped average cost curve which causes the perfectly competitive market to be uniformly distributed between firms, and it is for this reason that any firm can be called the 'representative agent'.

Static increasing returns
Increasing returns to scale represent positive feedback between firm size and firm efficiency: when s_i increases, c_i decreases. Learning by doing, network externalities and other phenomena leading to increasing returns allow early beginners to accumulate advantages and remain leaders. This positive feedback causes the selection of a particular equilibrium to be determined early on by small (random) events and the system to be characterized by 'multiple equilibria' and 'lock-in' (Arthur, 1990; David, 1985). Commonly cited examples which illustrate the selection of particular equilibrium points by early events include the competition between Qwerty and Dworak keyboards (David, 1985), VHS and Beta standards for video-cassette recorders (Arthur, 1990), and AM and FM radios. Geographic development has also been explained through positive

feedback mechanisms; Krugman (1979) claims that industrial development of the northeastern United States occurred because of the positive feedback experienced by early starters who were able to develop market networks. In international trade, forces of positive feedback have been used to explain the role of 'absolute' as opposed to 'comparative' advantage (Dosi et al., 1988).

To model increasing returns to scale, we substitute equation (2.3c) $(c_2 - c_1) = f(s_2 - s_1)$, into equation (2.3), where the function $f(f'(x) < 0)$ states that when s_1 increases, c_1 decreases. Since $s_1 + s_2 = 1$, we may write (2.3c) as

$$c_2 - c_1 = s_1 - s_2 = s_1 - (1 - s_1) = 2s_1 - 1,$$

which when plugged into equation (2.3) produces:

$$\dot{s}_1 = \lambda s_1(1 - s_1)(2s_1 - 1). \tag{2.6}$$

Figure 2.6 depicts the phase diagram for equation (2.6). The arrows indicate that the equilibrium point $(s_i = 1/n)$ is unstable. If market shares begin equal, any small perturbation in the vicinity of that equilibrium point will cause market shares to diverge from that point: if the small movement is to the left of $1/n$, then $s_1 \rightarrow 0$, while if it is to the right of $1/n$, then $s_1 \rightarrow 1$. The system is thus characterized by multiple equilibria, where the selection of a particular equilibrium depends on initial market shares.

The dynamics of increasing returns to scale and multiple equilibria, has been widely studied in the literature on path-dependency and network externalities

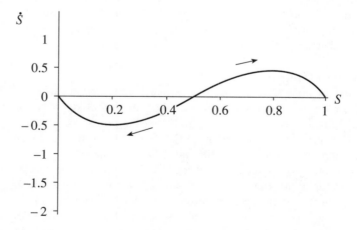

Figure 2.6   Static increasing returns to scale

(Arthur, 1990; David, 1994; Krugman, 1994) and is well represented by the quotation from Arthur (1994, p. 1) above. Marshall long ago argued that increasing returns to scale cause firm size to be unpredictable: 'whatever firm gets a good start, corners the market' (Marshall, 1948). The 'good start' could be a result of luck and other non-predictable early events. Such indeterminacy causes problems of uniqueness and stability for microeconomic theory (Sraffa, 1926). Brian Arthur's work has used polya-urn processes, Fokker–Planck equations and random walks to depict the dependence of the selected equilibrium on early events (Arthur, 1990).

Combination of different returns

As a last example of static returns to scale, we now incorporate both increasing and decreasing returns to scale dynamics in a single cost equation. Equation (2.3d) describes a polynomial cost function which embodies increasing returns to scale within one range of market shares (between 0 and $1/n$ and between $1/n$ and 1) and decreasing returns to scale within another range of market shares (between b and a)

$$c_2 - c_1 = (1 - 2s_1)(s_1 - a)(s_1 - b), \tag{2.3d}$$

substituting (2.3d) into (2.3):

$$\dot{s} = \lambda s_1 (1 - s_1)(1 - 2s_1)(s_1 - a)(s_1 - b),$$
$$\text{with } 1/2 < a < 1 \text{ and } 0 < b < 1/2. \tag{2.7}$$

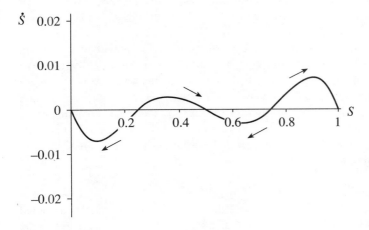

Figure 2.7   Combination of different returns to scale

Figure 2.7, the phase diagram for equation (2.7), illustrates that different initial market shares will lead to different long-term equilibria, setting $a = 3/4$, $b = 1/4$ and $\lambda = 1$. If s_1 begins between 0 and b, then $s_1 \to 0$; if s_1 begins between b and a then $s_1 \to 1/n$; and if s_1 begins between a and 1, then $s_1 \to 1$. The points b and a, are unstable equilibrium points since very small disturbances around those points will cause divergence from those points. The point $1/n$ is a stable equilibrium as long as perturbations are not very large.

4.2 Dynamic Economies of Scale

Having studied the relationship between size and direction of costs embodied in static returns to scale, we are now ready to study the feedback between size and the rate of cost reduction. The analysis of this *dynamic* returns to scale allows us to study the dynamics of innovation.

In exploring the feedback between market structure and innovation, we assume unit costs are always falling and the rate of cost reduction depends on scale. Positive feedback means that an increase in market share causes the firm's rate of cost reduction to increase (equation 2.9, below), while negative feedback means that an increase in market share causes the firm's rate of cost reduction to decrease (equation 2.8, below). In each of the simulations we assume that costs begin randomly distributed while market shares begin equally distributed ($s_i = 1/n$, $i = 1, ..., n$). Different variance levels of the initial distribution of costs (γ) are experimented with. The parameter γ is industry specific because it should be higher in industries where the underlying technological base is radically different from existing methods, as opposed to an industry which begins with the accumulated knowledge base from existing methods.

The model is kept simple so that a clear typology of market structures can match different market patterns with variations in empirically intuitive parameters. The parameters include the initial distribution of firm efficiencies (γ) and the industry-specific speed of cost reduction (α). We first model the case of negative feedback, then positive feedback, and then their combination in two versions of the life-cycle story. We compare the simulation results to results found in the empirical literature on the relationship between firm size, innovation and market structure.

Dynamic decreasing returns

Negative feedback between size and the rate of cost reduction is depicted through a differential equation (equation 2.8) for costs which illustrates that the speed of cost reduction of firm i falls as the market share of firm i increases:

$$\dot{c}_i = -\alpha(1 - s_i)c_i. \qquad (2.8)$$

Because of the logarithmic form of the equation, the parameter α determines the speed with which intra-industry costs converge to a minimum cost. It is an industry-specific parameter which can be interpreted as the strength of spillovers of knowledge and diffusion. The exact rate of cost reduction of any one firm depends both on the value of α as well as on its particular market share. The parameter α is an industry-specific parameter that can be interpreted either as the degree of technological opportunity (ease of innovation) in the industry or as the average rate of cost reduction in the industry. We prefer the latter interpretation. The exact rate of cost reduction of any one specific firm depends both on the value of α as well as on its market share via equation (2.1). The value of α might depend on the 'tacitness' of the knowledge base in an industry, on the patent system, and on other industry- and technology-specific factors which affect spillovers and diffusion (Pavitt, 1984).

Although in any given simulation run α is held constant so that we can look at the effect of varying its value in different runs, α could be made to evolve endogenously in the model. It could be made a function of the emergent level of concentration or instability, or it could change stochastically. For example, we might expect that when concentration is high (such as during the mature phase of an industry), the value of α is lower if concentration has a negative effect on innovation (Cohen and Levin, 1989; Scherer, 1984). We leave this experiment to a subsequent exploration of the model.

What would we expect a priori from a model of dynamic decreasing returns to scale? Intuition suggests that a turbulent 'switching' pattern of firm market shares might arise because when one firm gains a market share advantage, its costs begin to fall at a slower rate (equation 2.8) which cause it to be passed in market share by a smaller firm whose costs are falling at a faster rate (equation 2.1). The dynamic then repeats itself for the previously small, now growing firm. When equations (2.1) and (2.8) are simulated below, we see in fact that a 'switching' pattern emerges under certain parameter values.

The time path of market shares and costs with different values of α and a constant initial distribution of costs ($\gamma = 0.01$) are displayed in Figure 2.8. The replicator dynamic described in equation (2.1) causes market shares to stabilize once all costs have converged to the lowest possible cost.

For different values of the parameter α, very different market structures emerge; the size of α determines the speed at which all costs fall to a minimum level and hence the probability that the switching has time to take place. A very low value of α causes the inertia in costs to overwhelm the negative feedback dynamic and hence monopoly to emerge before switching takes place. This is similar to the case of simple selection. A very high α instead causes costs to fall so fast that the effect of convergence overwhelms the negative feedback

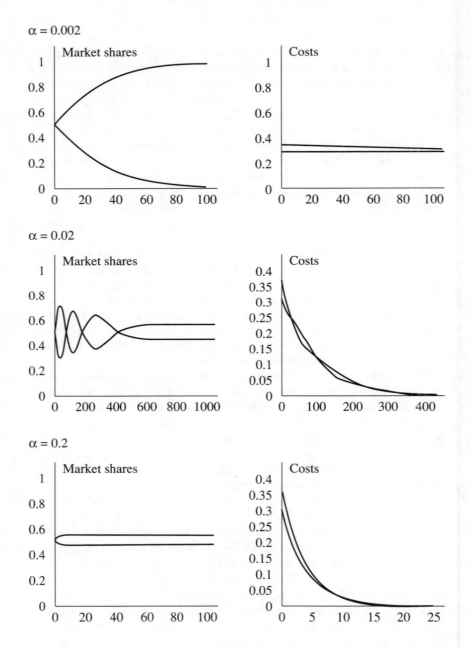

Figure 2.8   Equations (2.1) and (2.8) for n = 2, *γ* = 0.01 *and different* α

dynamic. Only when α is at an intermediate level does the instability that we predicted emerge: for values of α between 0.007 and 0.02, switching occurs with any initial distribution of costs. In this case future market shares are not predictable based on past market shares; the asymptotic leader is not necessarily the initially most efficient firm.

The connection between predictability and the underlying structure of production recalls Klein's (1977) hypothesis that market share patterns in industries or periods characterized by dynamic efficiency (that is, industries or periods in which firms benefit from exploring new technological frontiers) are

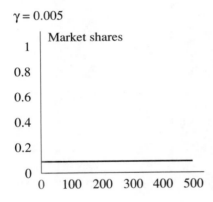

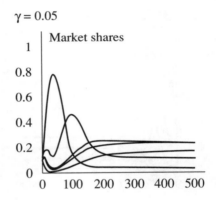

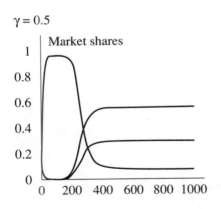

Figure 2.9   Equations (2.1) and (2.8) with n = 10, α = 0.02 *and different* γ

less predictable than those characterized by static efficiency (that is, industries
or periods in which firms benefit from *exploiting* given frontiers of production).

The higher the variance in the initial distribution of costs (γ), the more
turbulent is the market share instability. Figure 2.9 illustrates this for $n = 10$
firms,[6] $\alpha = 0.02$ (that is, in the switching range), and three different variance
levels ($\gamma = 0.005$, 0.05 and 0.5 with mean = 0.6). We see that a greater initial
dispersion of costs causes greater market share instability and more early exits
hence higher concentration. Figure 2.10 illustrates the complete results for one
particular case.

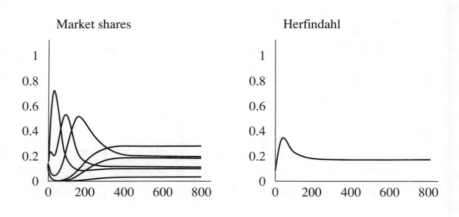

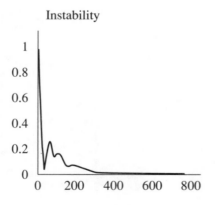

Figure 2.10   Equations (2.1) and (2.8) with n = 10, $\alpha = 0.02$ *and* $\gamma = 0.02$

The results are explained first verbally and then in table format in Table 2.1, below. Comparisons with empirical studies are highlighted in *italics*.

- For values of $\alpha < 0.002$ a *monopolistic* market emerges. This is because when costs change very slowly, selection forces completely dominate the evolutionary process allowing only the initially most fit firm to survive. Path-dependency exists since whichever firm happens to be the leader at $t = 0$ will remain the leader for ever. This is similar to the case of 'simple selection' in which future market shares can easily be predicted from knowledge of past market shares. *This result recalls empirical studies which find concentration to be more conducive to innovation in low 'technological opportunity' industries in which the science base moves relatively slowly and predictably (Comanor, 1967; Geroski, 1990; Scherer, 1984).*
- For parameter values $0.002 < \alpha < 0.007$, unit costs fall slowly but rapidly enough to allow partial *co-existence* of those firms $(< n)$ whose costs converge before the selection mechanism has time to force all laggard firms out of the industry. Firms with above-average costs exit early. No switching or turbulence occurs since with a low α, the forces of selection embodied in equation (2.1) are still stronger than the force of negative feedback.
- For parameter values $0.007 < \alpha < 0.03$, a *switching* pattern among market shares emerges. Negative feedback is strong enough to cause firms with high market shares to experience slower rates of cost reduction and thus to be surpassed in market share by smaller firms. The process causes switching to occur until all surviving firms' costs converge. For values of α closer to 0.03 the switching becomes so turbulent (increasing instability index) that more firms are forced to exit very early. An important result here is that, as opposed to the two extreme cases, the final ranking of firms is *unpredictable* since the initially most efficient firm does not necessarily become the industry leader. *This result recalls the empirical finding that market share turbulence tends to be higher during periods in which small firms have relative advantages in the innovative process, such as the early phase of the life-cycle (Abernathy and Wayne, 1974; Acs and Audretsch, 1987; Audretsch, 1995; Klein, 1977; Klepper, 1996; Tushman and Anderson, 1986).*
- When α is high, $\alpha > 0.03$, there is no switching since costs fall so fast that all firms reach the lowest possible cost before diseconomies of scale or selection have time to take effect. The early convergence allows all firms to co-exist and the firm with the initially lowest cost to be the final leader. The larger the value of α, the earlier market shares reach an equilibrium value. The final ranking of firms is predictable; firms rank according to

Firm size, innovation and market structure

their initial relative efficiency levels. *The last two results recall the empirical finding that in any given industry, market structure tends to be less concentrated in countries characterized by fast rates of innovation than in those characterized by low rates of innovation (see Dosi, 1984 for the case of semiconductors). They also recall the finding that small firms have a higher innovation/employee ratio than larger firms in 4-digit*

Table 2.1   Statistics describing simulation results for dynamic negative feedback

	α	Entropy	Var. shares	Herfindhal	Instability	Cumul ins.	Time conv.	N
$\gamma = 0.004$	0.002							
	0.02	1	0.0001	0.102	0.002	8.5	300	10
	0.05	0.99	0.0008	0.108	0.002	2.65	130	10
	0.1	1	0.0005	0.105	0.002	2.65	26	10
	0.2	1	0.0001	0.1012	0.002	1.03	17	10
	0.5	1	0.00002	0.1	0.002	0.4577	7	
$\gamma = 0.2$	0.002	0	0.089	1	0.002	21	60	1
	0.02	0.7	0.009	0.19	0.002	20	350	7
	0.05	0.75	0.011	0.21	0.002	17	180	6
	0.1	0.8	0.009	0.19	0.002	11	100	7
	0.2	0.9	0.005	0.163	0.002	6.5	35	10
	0.5	0.99	0.001	0.1	0.002	2.5	10	10
$\gamma = 0.4$	0.002	0.001	0.087	0.9	0.002	22.67	133	1
	0.02	0.5	0.1	0.35	0.002	21.84	500	4
	0.05	0.7	0.01	0.209	0.002	20.27	155	6
	0.1	0.78	0.011	0.21	0.002	9.57	42	7
	0.2	0.8	0.01	0.203	0.002	9.22	24	8
	0.5	0.99	0.001	0.116	0.002	3.44	10	10

Note: Table of results for negative feedback with different variance levels for the initial distribution of costs ($\gamma = 0.004$, 0.2, 0.4). Each value was calculated from an average of 50 simulation runs with a given value for alpha and for the variance of initial costs.

Time conv. (TC) = The time at which market shares reach a steady state; determined by when the instability Index reaches 0.002

N = Number of firms remaining at TC.

Entropy = $-\sum_{i=1}^{n} s_i \log s_i$, calculated at TC.

Herfindahl = $\sum_{i=1}^{n} s_i^2$, calculated at TC.

Instability = $\sum_{i=1}^{n} \left(\left|s_{i,t} - s_{i,t-1}\right|\right)$, calculated at TC.

Cumul. ins. = $\sum_{t=1}^{TC} I_t$, calculated at TC.

Var. shares = Variance of market shares, calculated at TC.

industries with high innovation rates (large α) (Acs and Audretsch, 1987) and that vigorous innovation has been found to be more concentration reducing than increasing (Geroski, 1990; Mukhopadhyay, 1985). Lastly, Lunn (1986) has found that while process innovation (incremental) tends to produce a concentrated market structure, product innovation (radical) tends to produce a more competitive market structure.

- When the simulation is run with different variance levels for the initial distribution of costs ($\gamma = 0.004$, 0.2 and 0.4, all with mean = 0.6), it is found that with any given value of α, the higher is the initial variance of costs, the longer it takes for market shares to reach an equilibrium value. And in the parameter range for which switching occurs ($0.007 < \alpha < 0.03$), it is found that a higher variance of initial costs, causes market shares to be more turbulent as measured by the (cumulative) instability index (column 6 in Table 2.1), which causes more early exits and hence a higher Herfindahl index (column 4 in Table 2.1). Thus in those industries in which the degree of variety between firm efficiencies is greater, there is a higher probability that market shares will be unstable over time, that concentration will be high, and that market shares take a longer time to reach a stable value. *Case-studies support this result through the finding that low levels of asymmetry in firm characteristics allow more firms to compete and the effect of convergence (imitation) to soften the power of selection, preventing a concentrated structure from emerging (Dosi and Orsenigo, 1987).*

Dynamic increasing returns

Dynamic increasing returns to scale refers to the case where an increase in market shares leads to an increase in the rate of cost reduction. Section 3, above, developed the economic foundation for this concept: as firms grow, their retained earnings allow them to spend more on R&D and on superior managers and engineers and hence to become better innovators. Equation (2.9) formalizes this dynamic:

$$\dot{c}_i = -\frac{1}{n-1}\alpha(s_i)c_i. \tag{2.9}$$

Since the average rate of cost reduction for equation (2.8) is equal to $-\alpha(n-1)$, while for equation (2.9) it is equal to $-\alpha$, the term $1/n-1$ in equation (2.9) serves to equalize the average rates of cost reduction in equations (2.8) and (2.9), eliminating any bias in the two equations and also rendering dimensionless (hence more easy to calibrate) the parameter α. When we simulate equations (2.1) and (2.9) for $n = 2$ firms and $\gamma = 0.01$, the time paths for market shares and costs are observed (see Figure 2.11). As in the negative feedback case, we see

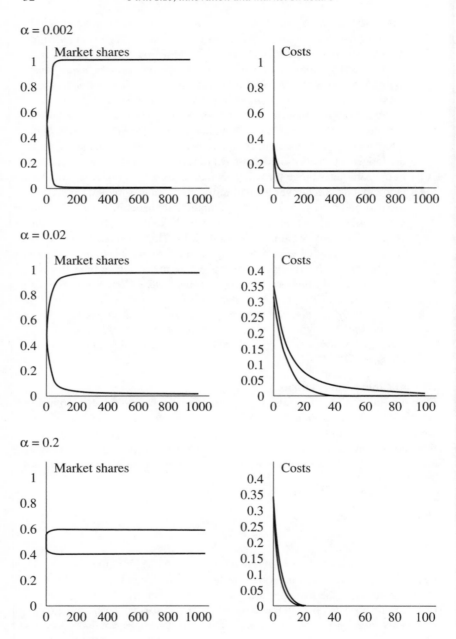

Figure 2.11   Equations (2.1) and (2.9) with n = 2, γ = 0.01 *and different* α

that a very slow speed of cost reduction ($\alpha = 0.002$) causes the selection mechanism to be so powerful that the initially most efficient firm captures the whole market. As mentioned above, this result confirms the empirical evidence that technologically laggard industries tend to be more concentrated. Also, as in the case of negative feedback, a fast rate of cost reduction ($\alpha = 0.2$) allows the force of convergence to outweigh the force of divergence. However, unlike the case of negative feedback, an intermediate rate of cost reduction ($\alpha = 0.02$) produces a market structure that is qualitatively simply somewhere in the middle of that which arises in the two extreme cases: no value of α causes a turbulent market structure to arise and firm ranking is *always predictable* given the initial relative efficiency levels. The exact degree of concentration is dependent on the parameter α and the initial cost distribution.

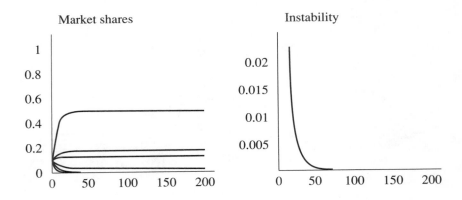

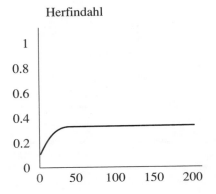

Figure 2.12   Dynamic increasing returns with $\alpha = 0.2$

Results from a simulation run for $n = 10$ firms are displayed in Figure 2.12; concentration increases monotonically while instability decreases monotonically. When we experiment with different variance levels for the initial distribution of costs, we see that regardless of the value of α that we choose, an increase in the initial variance of costs increases the level of market concentration. Figure 2.13 illustrates this for $n = 10$ firms with a constant value for α ($= 0.4$) and two different variance levels ($\gamma = 0.004$ and 0.2). The result that a higher initial variance in costs causes more early exits and hence a more concentrated market

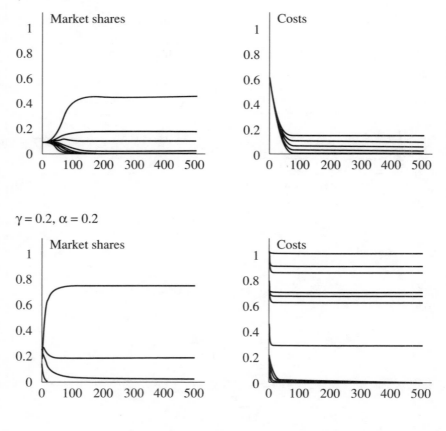

Figure 2.13   Equations (2.1) and (2.9) with n = 10, α = 0.2 and different γ (mean = 0.6)

structure to emerge was also found in the negative feedback case, but there the higher variance also caused the level of instability to increase.

Independently of the variance level and the speed of cost reduction parameter α, the case of dynamic increasing returns to scale always makes the firm with the initially lowest cost persist as the market leader. This path-dependent result where 'size begets size' was also found in the case of *static* increasing returns to scale (David, 1985, 1994) and in the case of dynamic decreasing returns with a very high or low value for α.

These results are summarized below. Since the simulation results with extreme values of α are very similar to those for negative feedback with such extreme values, we indicate the empirical counterparts only, with citations in parentheses.

- When the value of α is high (≥ 0.2), which means that firm costs are falling rapidly, firms reach a *stable co-existence*, with their ranking determined by the initial cost advantages. The higher is α, the less concentrated is the equilibrium market structure (as α increases, the Herfindahl index approaches $1/n$). This is similar to the negative feedback result with a high α. *(For empirical comparison, see: Acs and Audretsch, 1987; Geroski, 1990; Lunn, 1986.)*
- With low values of α (≤ 0.02), *only one firm survives* (as α decreases, the Herfindahl index approaches 1). This is also similar to the case of negative feedback. *(For empirical comparison, see: Comanor, 1967; Geroski, 1990; Scherer, 1984.)*
- Unlike the case of negative feedback with an intermediate value of α, positive feedback with an intermediate value leads simply to a market structure that is somewhere in between the result with a high and low α. The initially most fit firm always remains the market leader and the exact value of α determines how many other firms co-exist with the leader.
- With any given level of α, the higher is the variance in the initial distribution of costs, the more concentrated is the asymptotic market structure. *(For empirical comparison, see Dosi and Orsenigo, 1987.)*

Life-cycle I

We recall that the point of exploring the different feedback scenarios was to reproduce, and hence to better understand, regularities in different industries' market share patterns. The modeling procedure for simple selection and static decreasing returns was inspired by stories told in the case-study literature regarding the changing relationship between firm size and innovation. Figure 2.1 illustrated such patterns for the US automobile industry. Having explored the typology of market structures which arise from different feedback scenarios, we now combine the different types of feedback to study the effect of changes in 'innovation regimes'.

We first experiment with the hypothesis that negative feedback exists during the 'early' phase of the industry life-cycle, and positive feedback exists during the 'mature' phase of the industry life-cycle. The opposite is explored under 'life-cycle II', below, and can be interpreted as a third stage of the life-cycle in which a new product innovation causes there to be a reversal in the fortune of the leaders. Although we do not consider 'entry' dynamics, we embody the essence of the life-cycle argument in a cost equation which claims that small firms have a faster *rate of cost reduction* than large firms during the early phase of an industry (due to their greater flexibility and adaptability to the uncertain nature of the environment), while large firms have a faster rate of cost reduction during the 'mature' phase of an industry (due to the economies of scale in R&D, and the greater role of capital intensity in production). The economic foundation behind this hypothesis was reviewed in Section 3, above. We incorporate such dynamics into the model by choosing an arbitrary moment in industry history $t = t_x$ at which the existing type of feedback between costs and shares undergoes a change. For our first case we assume that equation (2.8) holds from $t = 0 - t_x$, and equation (2.9) holds from $t = t_x + 1 - tmax$ (the end of the simulation run).

The parameter t_x should be interpreted as an industry-specific parameter: a low t_x describes an industry in which the period of negative feedback lasts a short time because the product is standardized quickly, allowing economies of scale and the positive feedback regime to begin. Although here we focus on comparative static exercises with different values of t_x, it would clearly be interesting to make this switch point an *endogenous* variable. It could be made a function of the emergent level of concentration or instability. One might, for example, posit that once the Herfindahl index reaches a certain threshold point, large size becomes a barrier to innovation. However, for the purpose of the present analysis, in any given simulation run t_x is a constant parameter. Since there are various reasons why different industries should have different values of t_x (different time periods in which switches in regime occur), variations in its value in different runs allow us to explore hypothetically the dynamics in different industries.

Given the results of the simulation for the positive and negative feedback scenarios, we expect that for values of α around 0.05, the simulation of the above dynamic would lead to a semi-turbulent and competitive structure during the first stage of the life-cycle and to a partially or to a totally concentrated market structure during the second stage.

We first set $t_x = 150$ meaning that at $t = 150$ the industry goes from experiencing negative feedback to experiencing positive feedback between market shares and costs. Figure 2.14 confirms that this dynamic leads to a period of market share turbulence followed by a period of market concentration and market share stability. The figure shows that in the period of dynamic decreasing returns to scale, there is rising instability and increasing concentration. In contrast, in the dynamic increasing returns to scale period, instability falls and concentration rises.

Figure 2.15 illustrates the market share patterns that emerge with different values for t_x. The lower is t_x, the less relevant is the period of negative feedback, and hence the less turbulence.

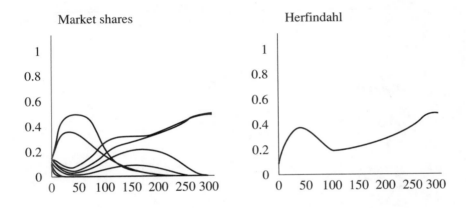

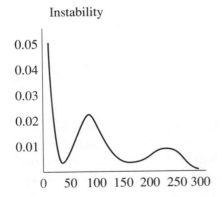

Figure 2.14   *Equation (2.8) from* t *= 0–150 and equation (2.9) from* t *= 150–300, with* α *= 0.02*

Market shares   Market shares

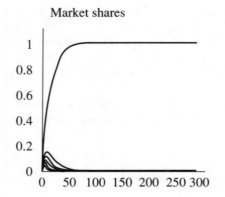   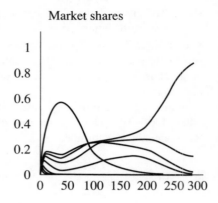

Market shares

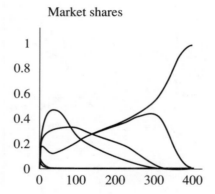

Figure 2.15   Same simulation as in Figure 2.14 with different values for
            t_x *(= 20, 200, 300)*

Life-cycle II

We now consider the opposite case: a switch from positive to negative feedback. We set t_x relatively low ($t_x = 20$) since if it is set too high then total monopoly will emerge very quickly and no firms will exist to experience the negative feedback phase. We experiment again with $\alpha = 0.02$ in order to produce instability in the negative feedback stage (see Figure 2.16). As expected from our earlier results, in the positive feedback phase ($t = 0$–20) the market is concentrated, while in the negative feedback phase ($t = 21$–300) the market is less concentrated and more turbulent.

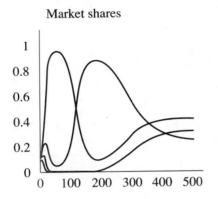

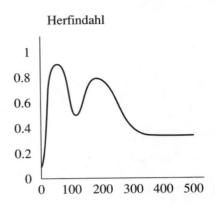

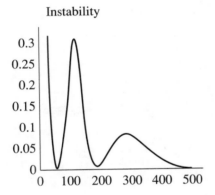

Figure 2.16 *Equation (2.9) from* t = 0–20 *and equation (2.8) from* t = 21–500, *with* α = 0.02

Figure 2.17 illustrates results from a simulation run with changes in t_x (clockwise: t_x = 30, 20, 10, 5). We see that the earlier the change in feedback regime occurs, the earlier the switching occurs and the more firms are able to survive the initial shakeout. This suggests that although industries go through both periods of negative and positive feedback, the shorter is the period of positive feedback and/or the longer is the period of negative feedback, the greater number of firms co-exist and the less concentrated is the market.

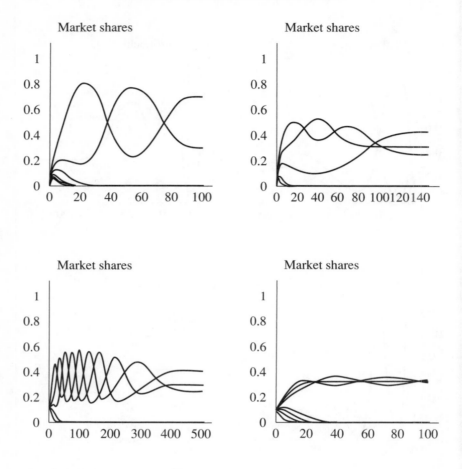

*Figure 2.17   Equation (2.9) with $\alpha = 0.2$ and equation (2.8) with $\alpha = 0.02$;
different t_x (clockwise = 30, 20, 10, 5)*

5   COMPARISON OF SIMULATION RESULTS TO EMPIRICAL DATA IN THE US AUTOMOBILE INDUSTRY

The simulation exercise allowed us to explore the implications of different theories regarding firm size and innovation on the evolution of market structure. The type of positive and negative feedback described by authors studying the automobile industry, such as Abernathy and Wayne (1974) in their discussion

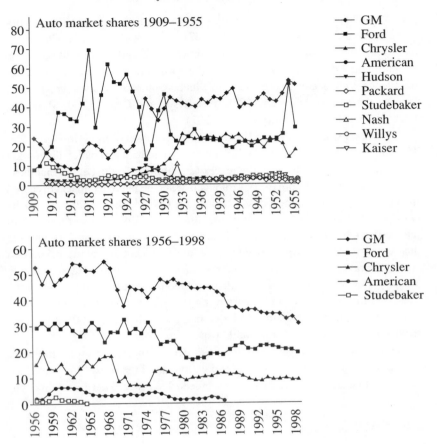

Figure 2.18   Different degrees of market share instability in the US auto industry

of the 'limits to the learning curve' and Klein (1977) in his discussion of 'static efficiency' versus 'dynamic efficiency', is very similar to that described by our notion of dynamic increasing and decreasing returns to scale; high increases in volume through specialization cause the *rate of cost reduction* to fall during periods of technological and market uncertainty and to rise during periods of market and technological stability . These authors suggest that in the history of the US automobile industry we find that periods which have been characterized by little pressure for innovation (for example, the period of mass production between 1908 and 1924, and the 1980s) resulted in more stability and concentration in market shares; while periods characterized by strong innovation and uncertainty (for example, the pioneering period 1890s–1908, and the immediate post-Model T period 1924–late1940s) led to more market share instability (Abernathy and Wayne, 1974; Klein, 1977).[7] As already stated in Chapter 1, the results in these studies are similar to those found in the recent literature on 'technological discontinuities' and 'architectural innovation', where industry turbulence is connected to the degree to which an innovation disrupts the status quo (Tushman and Anderson, 1986; Henderson and Clark, 1990; Markides, 1998; Hamel, 1998; and Christensen, 1997).

The market share patterns in Figure 2.18 are a subset of those in Figure 2.1. They illustrate two periods in the US automobile industry in which the market share patterns clearly differ in the level of instability. To the degree that these patterns are generated from the type of positive and negative feedback discussed in Abernathy and Wayne (1974) and Klein (1977), these patterns can be compared to those which emerge in our 'life-cycle' simulations of a switch in the feedback between firm size and innovation. Figures 2.18 and 2.19 provide this comparison. The purpose is not to 'test' the model but to provide insight into some general processes leading to market share changes in the US automobile industry. Figure 2.19 displays the patterns from one typical simulation run of the life-cycle I model, where a first period ($t = 0$–100) of negative feedback leads to a turbulent market structure, and a second period ($t = 101$–400) of positive feedback leads to a more stable market structure.

The simulation exercise permitted us to deepen the above propositions by asking under what conditions these predictions hold the most. We found, for example, that negative feedback does indeed lead to market instability, but

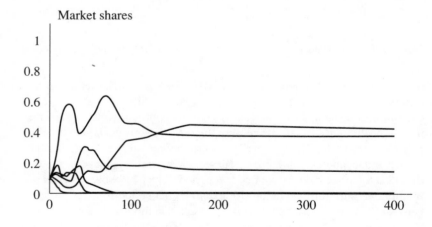

Figure 2.19   Life-cycle I: negative $\Rightarrow$ positive feedback

only when the industry average rate of cost reduction is neither too high nor too low.

It should be noted, however, that not all life-cycle theorists believe that the instability in market shares characteristic of the early period in the industry life-cycle arises due to dynamic decreasing returns. Klepper and Graddy (1990) and Klepper (1996), in opposition to Abernathy and Wayne (1974) and Klein (1977), claim that instability in market shares emerges not from dynamic decreasing returns to scale but from the existence of idiosyncratic events during periods of dynamic *increasing returns to scale*. In Chapter 3, we explore this hypothesis in a stochastic version of the model presented above.

6   CONCLUSION AND DISCUSSION

The chapter presented a model in which market share patterns emerge from the feedback between firm size and innovation. Results from this type of *Gendanken* experiment are not meant to represent the detailed dynamics of any particular industry or firm, but to produce a general typology linking cost/innovation dynamics to market share patterns. The model was purposefully kept simple so to (1) analyse systematically the effect of different feedback mechanisms between firm costs and market shares (scale) in isolation from other factors such as oligopolistic pricing, elasticity of demand, and entry; and (2) to allow the market share dynamics which emerge from the simulation to be traced to variations in (few) parameters which have empirical relevance. The first reason was deemed particularly important since the emergence of path-dependency and disequilibrium dynamics from *negative* feedback processes is relatively unexplored (as opposed to the now numerous and very interesting studies on the generation of multiple equilibria from *positive* feedbacks in the economy); and the second reason was deemed important since it allows a typology of market share patterns to be constructed from the variation of empirically motivated firm-specific parameters (for example, firm size) and industry-specific parameters (for example, average speed of innovation, initial degree of variety between firms).

Having uncovered some *non-intuitive* general properties of the deterministic dynamics, the ground is now clear for the possible introduction of more firm- and industry-specific factors. The flexibility of the model, and the fact that it does not depend on restrictive behavioral assumptions, renders it open to such additions and modifications (motivated again by empirical case studies). For example, the parameter denoting the speed of market share adjustment (λ) in equation (2.1) as well as the parameter denoting the industry-specific average rate of cost reduction (α) could be made to evolve endogenously with the changing Herfindahl index and/or instability index; a rising level of market concentration can affect the speed at which costs adjust to shares and/or the speed at which shares adjust to costs (or other measures of 'fitness'). The time period in the industry life-cycle in which a change in feedback regime occurs, t_x, could also be made to evolve endogenously with the changing market structure (the period of negative feedback might depend on the level of concentration or on the level of instability).

Stochastic shocks can be introduced to represent the idiosyncratic nature of decisions and outcomes concerning production and innovation. A crucial element to any study of production and innovation is the uncertain trial-and-error aspect of the development of technology, of product marketing and of everyday production decisions. By introducing a stochastic element to costs we can see how the deterministic results are altered; does dynamic increasing returns to scale still result in the leadership of the initially most fit firm and how does the ability of firms to adapt to shocks *differ* in the different phases of the life-cycle? These questions are addressed in Chapter 3.

To conclude, we review the principal results of the simulation model presented in this chapter, with empirical connections again in *italics*:

- When firm costs fall *very slowly*, determined by a low industry average rate of cost reduction (inertia), the market structure in *both* the cases of positive and negative feedback tends to be concentrated. If costs are falling *very rapidly*, the market structure tends to be less concentrated due to the quick convergence of inter-firm costs. In both these cases, the ranking of firms is *predictable*: the asymptotic leader is always the firm that was initially the most fit. In the very slow case, the force of selection overpowers the feedback mechanism causing costs to change; while in the very fast case the speed with which costs change overpowers both the effect of selection as well as the mechanism causing costs to change. *The first result seems to coincide with empirical studies which have found that markets tend to be more concentrated in industries with a low rate of innovation or, in the case of a given industry, in countries which are not leaders in innovation (Comanor, 1967; Dosi, 1984). The second result coincides with empirical studies which find that small firms are more able to become market leaders in industries with very fast rates of innovation (Geroski, 1990; Scherer and Ross, 1990; Acs and Audretsch, 1987).*

- When costs fall at an *intermediate* speed, positive feedback causes the emergent market structure to lie somewhere in between the very fast and very slow case. Negative feedback instead produces complex dynamics very different from the extreme cases. Such complexity takes the form of turbulence in market shares (instability and changes in rank) since larger firms are continuously surpassed in share by smaller firms with faster rates of cost reduction. In this case, it is *not possible to predict* future market shares based on current market shares. *This result coincides with empirical studies which find that uncertain environments, and environments in which small firms innovate more than large firms, tend to be characterized by more market share turbulence than certain environments and environments in which large firms innovate more (Abernathy and Wayne, 1974; Klein, 1977; Tushman and Anderson, 1986; Markides, 1998; Christensen, 1997.*

- For each type of feedback, and with any industry average rate of cost reduction, the higher is the variance of the initial distribution of costs, the more concentrated is the asymptotic market structure. In the case of negative feedback with an intermediate industry average rate of cost reduction, a higher initial cost variance also causes market shares to be more turbulent. The initial variance of costs is industry specific since it may be higher in industries where the underlying technology base is *radically* different from existing methods, as opposed to an industry that begins with the accumulated knowledge base of other methods. *This result is comparable to empirical studies which have shown that low levels of asymmetry in firm characteristics cause a less concentrated market to develop (Dosi and Orsenigo, 1987).*

- In the 'life-cycle' case, where we embody both positive and negative feedback in the cost equation, the emergent market structure is characterized by a relatively high degree of concentration and stability in the region of positive feedback, and by a relatively high degree of instability (and varying concentration) in the negative feedback region. The exact pattern depends on the industry average speed of cost reduction in each phase, the time period in which the 'change in regime' occurs, and the initial inter-firm cost variance. *The alternating periods of instability and concentration which emerge are similar to those reported in industry life-cycle studies (Abernathy and Utterback, 1975; Klein, 1977; Gort and Klepper, 1982; Klepper, 1996).*

These results allow us to confront the following questions: 'Given what we know about the mix of cost-reduction strategies in a particular industry (for example, economies of scale, necessity for flexible adaptation to uncertainty, vigorous innovation and so on) and the nature of the environment (for example, uncertain demand, changing technological standards), how would we expect market share patterns to evolve in that industry? How well do such predictions perform?'. The differing levels of predictability may be a factor which influences economic actions such as government industrial policy as well as the degree to which the stock market weighs the current 'fundamentals' of a particular firm. We explore this last question in Chapter 4. In the next chapter we explore the effect of idiosyncratic events on the dynamics explored above.

NOTES

*   The first part of this chapter is from 'Economies of scale during the industry life-cycle: a
     replicator dynamics framework', Santa Fe Institute Working Paper (1997–06–054). The second
     part is from 'A computational model of economies of scale and market share instability',
     Structural Change and Economic Dynamics, 1998, Vol. 9: 55–83, reprinted here with permission
     from Elsevier-Science.

1.   An exception is found in Winter and Rothblum (1985), where the skewed size distribution of
     firms and market share fluctuations are addressed together. The authors build a stochastic
     growth model which follows Gibrat's assumptions and show that although there is a tendency
     toward increasing market concentration while sample paths for individual firms fluctuate from
     very high to very low market shares (from near monopoly to near extinction). They claim that
     the reason why there is so much emphasis on concentration rather than on fluctuation is that
     the latter is very slow and hence unrecognizable in the short period. Although their model is
     one of the few that addresses both changing concentration and turbulence, they too rely only
     on random factors to explain these regularities rather than on intuition regarding underlying
     economic processes.

2.   As mentioned below, some life-cycle theorists focus solely on the area of positive feedback
     (dynamic increasing returns to scale) and claim that the turbulence comes from idiosyncratic
     random events, not from a period of negative feedback. The modeling framework used here
     considers both types of feedback while also leaving room for the exploration of the effect of
     random events.

3.   'What we have got to accept is that (the large-scale establishment) has come to be the most
     powerful engine of progress' (Schumpeter, 1942, p. 106).

4.   They find, for example, that the innovation rate is higher for large firms in the tire, chemical,
     industrial machinery and food machinery industries, while it is relatively higher for the small
     firms in the scales and balances, computing equipment, control instruments, and synthetic
     rubber industries (Acs and Audretsch, 1987).

5.   This is similar to the prediction in standard microeconomic theory that in the absence of
     diminishing returns, and/or in the presence of imperfect competition the leading firm will
     maintain its 'rent' and monopolize the industry.

6.   When there are only two firms it does not make sense to specify the variance of the initial cost
     distribution. In that case we draw from a uniform distribution with a specific range and vary
     the range in the different runs. With $n = 10$ firms we draw initial costs from a normal distrib-
     ution with a specified mean and variance.

7.   We note some important phases in the history of the auto industry: (1) In the pioneering phase
     (1890s–1908) the uncertainty of technology, product and demand created much instability in
     market shares due to the importance of flexibility and exploration in discovering new techniques.
     This was a period of decreasing returns to specialization. (2) The advent of Ford's Model T and
     the system of mass production (1909–24) allowed economies of scale to emerge where there
     were rewards, in terms of cost competitiveness and market share, to exploitation of existing
     techniques. This period of dynamic increasing returns caused the market to become more con-
     centrated and stable. (3) When, around 1925, the market experienced an upheaval due to
     consumers' new taste for a closed body comfortable car, firms 'locked into' the system of
     specialized mass production were not able to adapt flexibly to the new conditions. This created
     a period of market share instability where inflexible firms were penalized with large drops in
     market shares. Since the Second World War, periods of market share concentration and stability
     have been characteristic of periods of low innovation (Abernathy and Wayne, 1974, p. 114).

3. The effect of idiosyncratic events on the feedback between firm size and innovation: a stochastic analysis

1 INTRODUCTION

The validity of using a deterministic model to understand industrial dynamics comes into serious question when we are confronted with the increasing empirical and theoretical literature on the role of initial conditions and idiosyncratic events in influencing industry dynamics (Arthur, 1990; Klepper and Graddy, 1990). An idiosyncratic event is an event that could not have been predicted beforehand due to its local and non-structural nature. For example, Henry Ford's personality *did* influence the market structure of the US automobile industry and its existence surely could not have been predicted beforehand.

This chapter explores a stochastic version of the model presented in Chapter 2 with the aim of capturing the effect of uncertainty faced by firms in their production and innovation activities, and the strong penalties in market shares which they undergo when not able to adapt to change or when bad decisions are made. As in Chapter 2, the goal is to construct a simple model that allows us to explore the dynamics of firm size and innovation by varying a small set of parameters which have proved significant in the empirical literature. A direct comparison is made between the results that emerge from the deterministic and the stochastic versions of the model.

2 RANDOMNESS IN ECONOMIC MODELS

Although economic models increasingly embody stochastic components in the form of shocks, the precise effect of these components on the models is not always clear. This is either because the shocks in reality have no qualitative role beyond adding some noise around a deterministic trend (for example, in econometric models), or because the role of the shocks is so strong that it prevents the model from having much economic significance. Furthermore, when shocks are applied to a system characterized by non-linearity, this disguises whether the properties that emerge from the model (for example, turbulence, instability) are results of the underlying non-linear behavior or due to the stochastic shocks.

What does it mean for an economic model to contain a random component? Since not even economists believe that the world is free of errors, shocks and idiosyncratic events, economic models often include random variables to capture this aspect of everyday reality and/or to admit that the underlying model does not provide a full explanation of the independent variable. The method and philosophy, however, with which randomness is included differs between models. In some models, randomness is incorporated solely to account for the 'error' around a systematic trend, that is, a deviation around average behavior where it is the properties of the latter which are the focus of attention. Normally distributed random terms in econometric models have exactly this purpose, allowing the model to embody:

> a systematic component or true value and an 'erratic component' or 'disturbance' or 'accidental error'. The systematic components are assumed to satisfy the regression equation exactly ... the erratic component is taken as error in the literal sense of the word. (Koopmans, 1937, p. 5)[1]

Another use of randomness in economics can be found in theories of firm growth (for example, based on a Gibrat process) and theories of real business cycles. Here, randomness in the form of exogenous shocks is not used to create noise around an underlying trend but rather to account for the *total* growth of the system; that is, without exogenous shocks, the system would not leave its steady state. Such use of randomness can be criticized for hiding the *economic* causes of growth in a 'black box'. Ironically, such full reliance on randomness ignores not only the underlying causes of growth, but also the specific role of the random components themselves. And, as stated in Geroski et al. (1997, p. 171), the idea that market structure is a result of random factors 'may be more an artifact of the models than of the data itself'.

The philosophy behind both these approaches, that is, randomness to account for *noise* around mean behavior and randomness to account for *all change* is different from the use of randomness in evolutionary models. Evolutionary models in economics, whether stochastic or deterministic, focus on the origin and evolution of variety in a population of agents and the selection mechanism which winnows in on the variety. The system is driven partly by structural forces, resembling laws of motion, and partly by the social and idiosyncratic nature of the actors. The latter are not viewed as rational maximizers but as agents who adapt (whether successfully or not) through 'routines' and rules of thumb resembling more a 'satisficing' behavior than a 'maximizing' one (Nelson and Winter, 1982; Simon, 1984). The co-evolution of 'chance' and 'necessity' prevents the economic system from being deterministic and predictable:

> The patterns of evolution of the system are determined by the interaction between structural constraints (such as technological asymmetries between firms) and behavioral degrees of freedom of each economic agent. Nelson and Winter's model suggests a theory of evolution as a function of the behavioral regularities. We shall be essentially concerned with the evolution of the structural boundaries of these degrees of behavioral freedom. ... Whenever economic agents are able to change their environment and to choose within a limited set of alternative strategies, a strictly deterministic theory is impossible. Strategic freedom however, is not boundless and our model will focus on the evolving relationship between the range of possible performance outcomes and the nature of structural constraints. (Dosi, 1984, p. 11)

Stochastic concepts in this framework have a *qualitative* effect on the model, beyond adding 'noise', interacting with the underlying structural (economic and socio-political) mechanisms. They capture the idiosyncratic and novel patterns of interaction between heterogeneous agents that cannot be predicted a priori by theory and also interact with the underlying structural dynamics (for example, increasing returns to scale). These interactions along with external forces create a state of the world, which then influences the patterns of interaction, limiting the degree of freedom of the latter.

In a non-linear system, initial conditions determined by idiosyncratic events can have a strong influence on the final market outcome. An empirical example, reviewed in more detail below, can be found in Klepper and Graddy (1990) where regularities concerning entry, exit and concentration are reproduced in a model which emphasizes how random factors governing the early evolution of industries may shape their market structure at maturity:

> chance events and exogenous factors that influence the number of potential entrants to the industry, the growth rate of incumbent firms, and the ease of imitation of the industry leaders will influence the ultimate number and size distribution of firms in the industry. (Klepper and Graddy, 1990, p. 27)

This work is close to that of Arthur (1990), where interaction between positive feedback and random events is emphasized:

> In the real world, if several similar-size firms entered a market at the same time, small fortuitous events – unexpected orders, chance meetings with buyers, managerial whims – would help determine which ones achieved early sales and, over time, which firm dominated. Economic activity is quantified by individual transactions that are too small to observe, and these small 'random' events can accumulate and become magnified by positive feedbacks so as to determine the eventual outcome. These facts suggest(ed) that situations dominated by increasing returns should be modeled not as static deterministic problems but as dynamic processes based on random events and natural positive feedbacks, or non-linearities. (Arthur, 1990, p. 5)

Under such conditions, it is impossible to know a priori which of many different possible market structures will emerge in any given run. Rather, one can only: 'record the particular set of random events leading to each solution and study the probability that a particular solution would emerge under a set of initial conditions' (Arthur, 1990, p. 5)

3   INDUSTRY-SPECIFIC NATURE OF MARKET SHARE INSTABILITY

The model presented in Chapter 2 was compared to an industry life-cycle story which emphasizes a 'switch' in regime from negative feedback between size and innovation to positive feedback. The model presented in this chapter can be compared to a different life-cycle story which emphasizes the effect of random events on positive feedback dynamics. Before entering into the details of the model, we review these two life-cycle stories below.

Chapter 2 developed a deterministic model of *dynamic* economies of scale: the relationship between firm size and innovation. By deterministic we mean that there were no stochastic elements. The model is consistent with a particular theory of the life-cycle which claims that changes in market share patterns can be interpreted in terms of a 'switch' in regime from one type of feedback between firm size and innovation to another. As discussed in Chapter 2, Klein (1977), claims that it was a switch from 'dynamic' to 'static' efficiency which caused market share instability to decline in the US automobile industry. He claims that market share instability is more typical of periods in which firms compete based on dynamic efficiency, while market share stability is more typical of periods in which firms compete based on static efficiency. In periods of dynamic efficiency, the existence of uncertainty prevents optimal tradeoffs to be known beforehand, rendering decisions based on 'perfect knowledge' irrational. This view is similar to that found in Abernathy and Wayne (1974), where it is claimed that the changing nature of market patterns in the US auto industry resulted from the changing nature of demand and technology, which no longer made the learning curve, based on economies of scale, a profitable strategy to pursue. In explaining the changes in market shares that resulted from Ford's failure to adapt to changing demand conditions, they state: 'the highly specialized production process lacked the balance to handle the new product … management needs to recognize that conditions stimulating innovation are different from those favoring efficient, high-volume, established operations' (Abernathy and Wayne 1974, pp. 116, 118).

Another theory of the life-cycle is that found in Klepper and Graddy (1990) and Klepper (1996). In this view, it is not switches in regime that cause different types of market instability and concentration to emerge but rather the effect of random events on the process of positive feedback. It is assumed that there is always *positive* feedback between size and innovation but that this does not lead to a monotonic increase in concentration due to the effect of randomly distributed innovation capabilities and timing of entry, which cause the early stage of the industry to be characterized by market share instability. This initial instability in market shares later declines as the increase in output causes price–cost margins to fall and, consequently, some firms to exit (and entry to decrease). The latter occurs because the fall in price–cost margins lowers firm incentives to grow, given the related costs of adjustment. It is random events and positive feedback that determine who gets ahead early on and thus who survives the shakeout: 'chance events and exogenous factors that influence the number of potential entrants to the industry, the growth rate of incumbent firms, and the ease of imitation of the industry leaders will influence the ultimate number and size distribution of firms in the industry' (Klepper and Graddy, 1990, p. 27).

4   MODELING THE EFFECT OF IDIOSYNCRATIC EVENTS ON POSITIVE/NEGATIVE FEEDBACK

In what follows, the different feedback regimes explored in Chapter 2 are tested for how robust they are to stochastic shocks. Given the results in the deterministic analysis, we should expect the turbulence produced by the phase of dynamic negative feedback to be more sensitive to shocks than the phase of dynamic positive feedback since even without shocks the industry structure and ranking of firms which emerges from negative feedback is unpredictable (with an intermediate α). The market structure generated from positive feedback is probably more resistant to shocks since the force of selection is strongly biassed towards the initially most efficient firm. Yet the presence of shocks should prevent, at least in the beginning, any one firm from getting too far ahead of other firms.

As in Chapter 2, we begin the simulations with n firms that have equal market shares but randomly distributed costs. Firm market shares evolve according to the replicator dynamic of equation (2.1):

$$\dot{s}_i = \lambda \cdot s_i(\bar{c} - c_i), \, i = 1, \dots, n \tag{2.1}$$

$$\bar{c} \equiv \sum_i c_i s_i = \text{weighted average cost, where } \sum_i s_i = 1. \tag{2.1a}$$

As in equations (2.8) and (2.9), firm costs are assumed to always fall and the rate of cost reduction to depend on firm size. To examine the effect of a stochastic component on this type of dynamic economies of scale, we add a shock to equations (2.8) and (2.9):

$$\frac{\dot{c}_i}{c_i} = -\alpha(1 - s_i)\varepsilon_i \tag{3.1}$$

$$\frac{\dot{c}_i}{c_i} = -\frac{1}{n-1}\alpha(s_i)\varepsilon_i \tag{3.2}$$

where ε_i is an iid random variable drawn, at each moment in time for each firm i, from a normal distribution with mean = 1. To study the effect of different size shocks on the model, we vary the variance level (σ) of this distribution. We experiment with values $\sigma = 0$, 0.05, 0.1 and 0.2. If, for example, we increase σ from 0.05 to 0.1, this means that the possible size of the shocks has increased although at any moment in time the shock might be small.

For each size shock, the simulations are run with a given initial distribution of costs with mean 1 and variance γ and with a given speed of cost adjustment parameter (α). For each set of parameters, the results from 50 simulation runs are documented. The results are presented both graphically as well as through tables. While the graphs serve to illustrate 'typical' patterns from the simulations, the tables document the average statistics from the 50 runs with each set of parameters. For each set of parameters (α, γ, σ), we first calculate the time period (TC) in which market shares settle down to a constant value. This is determined by the period in which the instability index (defined in Chapter 1) reaches the value 0.002. The following data is then calculated at that time period: the Herfindahl index (HI2), the cumulative instability index (II2: the integral of the instability index from $t = 0$–TC), the surviving number of firms (n), and the number of times the ranking between firms changed (R). The value of the instability index and the Herfindahl index at the mid-way point (TC/2) are also calculated (under the headings II1 and HI1). The values in the table for each of these statistics correspond to the *average* value that emerges from 50 simulation runs using the same set of parameters. Turbulence in market structure is portrayed through the combination of the instability index and the number of times firm ranking changes. The latter has been used by Gort (1963).

For each simulation we display four graphs; the first displays the market shares for the whole simulation run; the second displays market shares for a shorter time period so that the path of very early market share dynamics is more evident; the third displays the evolution of concentration through the changing Herfindahl index; and the fourth displays the evolution of turbulence through the changing instability index. We always begin with the deterministic case for comparison. The economic interpretation of the results and a comparison of the results to those in similar studies (Arthur, 1990; Klepper and Graddy, 1990) are left to the conclusion in Section 5.

4.1 Stochastic Dynamic *Increasing* Returns to Scale

Whereas the deterministic simulation of the two different types of feedback allowed us to explore the hypothesis regarding innovation and instability found in Abernathy and Wayne (1974), Klein (1977) and Tushman and Anderson (1986), adding shocks to the positive feedback scenario allows us to explore the life-cycle hypothesis described in Klepper (1996) and the path-dependent dynamics described in Arthur (1990). Both of these hypotheses state that early turbulence in market shares can result from the effect of idiosyncratic events on increasing returns. Although positive feedback will eventually cause a concentrated market to emerge, shocks will prevent this from happening monotonically.

We add a stochastic component to the case of positive feedback with the objective of observing whether and how the results found in the deterministic simulation of dynamic positive feedback (Figure 2.1, above) are altered. We begin again with the case of a low industry average rate of cost reduction. We recall that in the deterministic case, a very low α (inertia in costs) causes the force of selection to dominate industry evolution and thus the Herfindahl index to always equal 1 and the firm with the initially lowest cost to *predictably* always become the market leader.

Figure 3.1 illustrates the market patterns which emerge from stochastic dynamic positive feedback with a relatively low value of α (= 0.002), a low variance of the initial cost distribution and different size shocks ($\sigma = 0, 0.05, 0.1, 0.2$). We see that in the stochastic positive feedback case, with a low value of α, it is still a concentrated market structure which emerges (as in the deterministic positive feedback case), yet the *process* towards concentration is not smooth as in the deterministic case but instead turbulent (in the deterministic case it was only with negative feedback and with a mid-level value for α that turbulence arose). It is thus not possible to know *ex ante* which firm will become the market leader.

Table 3.1, below, illustrates that a *mid-size* shock ($\sigma = 0.1$) with a low α causes the most turbulence and least concentration (CI2 = 2.48, 4.04, 2.6; R = 2.3, 5.3, 3, HI2 = 0.98, 0.86, 0.87). Instability first increases with shocks because the existence of shocks disrupts the force of selection caused by positive feedback. But if the shock is too big, turbulence decreases and concentration increases because the degree to which one firm can get shocked upwards or

(a) α = 0.002, γ = 0.1, no shock

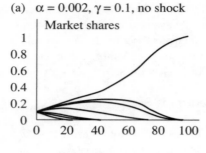

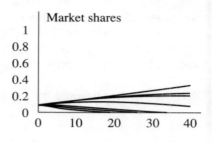

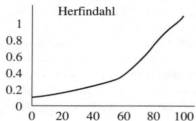

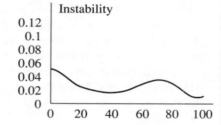

(b) α = 0.002, γ = 0.1, σ = 0.05

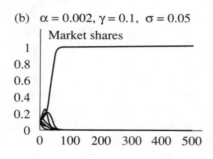

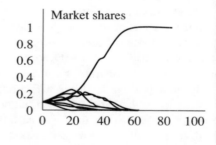

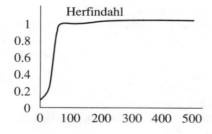

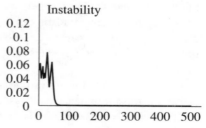

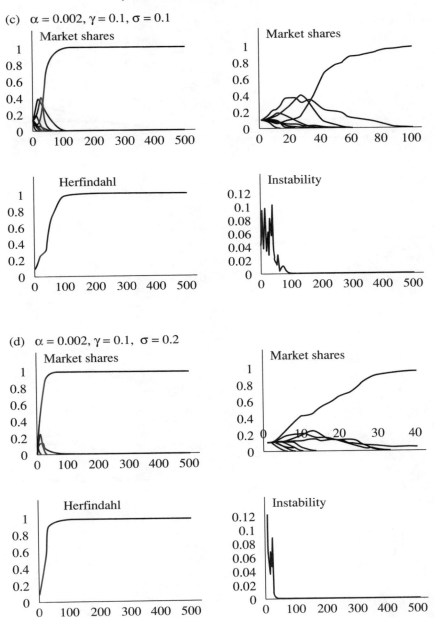

Figure 3.1 Stochastic increasing returns with α = 0.002, γ = 0.1 and different σ

(a) $\alpha = 0.02$, $\gamma = 0.1$, no shock

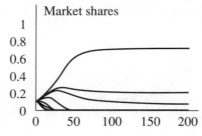

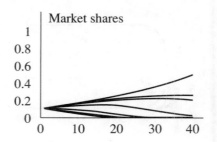

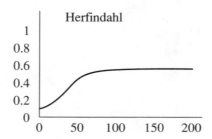

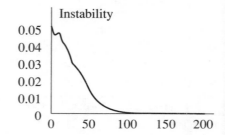

(b) $\alpha = 0.02$, $\gamma = 0.1$, $\sigma = 0.05$

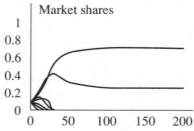

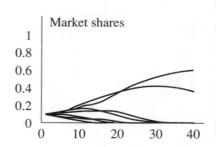

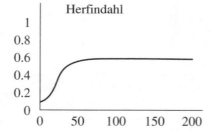

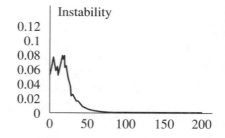

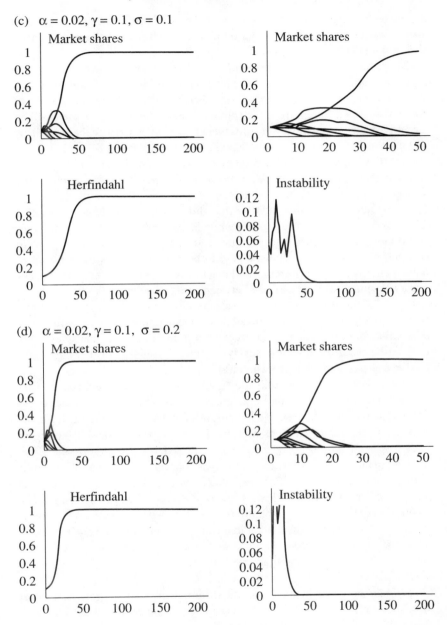

(c) α = 0.02, γ = 0.1, σ = 0.1

(d) α = 0.02, γ = 0.1, σ = 0.2

Figure 3.2   Stochastic increasing returns with α = 0.002, γ = 0.1 and different σ

downwards is larger and hence so is the shakeout of firms. The mid-size shock also produces the longest time period before which market shares settle to a steady state (TC = 63, 161, 76).

Except for the case of the very large shock, a higher variance of the initial cost distribution ($\gamma = 0.2$) causes the level of instability to be lower than with a lower variance level ($\gamma = 0.1$). This is because the higher is the degree to which firms are different from each other at the beginning, the stronger will be the early shakeout and the fewer firms there will be to experience the instability, and the shorter the time period in which the instability lasts (TC = 63, 161, 76 versus TC = 44, 43.5, 58). This might be because the higher initial variance in firm efficiencies makes the market structure less vulnerable to shocks due to the stronger force of selection.

To conclude, the results indicate that shocks applied to dynamic positive feedback with a low industry average rate of cost reduction α (or technological opportunity), cause the smooth and monotonic movement toward concentration in the deterministic case to be replaced with a more turbulent movement toward concentration, and that this is most true for *mid*-size shocks and a low initial level of variance between firm efficiencies.

Figure 3.2 illustrates the simulation results with a higher industry average rate of cost reduction: $\alpha = 0.02$. We recall that in the deterministic case with a mid-level value for α, the final market structure is more competitive than with a very low α (that is, more than one surviving firm) but that firm ranking is still predictable (no market share switching).

As was found in the deterministic case for both types of feedback, a faster average rate of cost reduction in the industry makes the market structure less concentrated than in the case of a lower level (compare the values of HI2 in the first, second and third columns of Table 3.1, below). Although the emergent market structure is always relatively concentrated, the shocks have the effect of creating turbulence in the process towards concentration. Yet unlike the case with a small α (Figure 3.1, above), shocks with a mid-size α *increase* the number of surviving firms. This is because the larger α causes selection to be much weaker than in the case of strong inertia (low α). As before, an increase in the shock size causes the market to be more concentrated (HI2 = 0.82, 0.84, 0.90) due to the effect of large shocks on the shakeout of firms. As in the case with a small value of α, the market evolution is most turbulent with mid-size shocks (CI2 = 2.08, 2.37, 2.04 ; R = 1.5, 5, 4).

A higher variance in the initial distribution of costs causes the market structure, with a given value of α and σ, to be less concentrated (HI2 = 0.514, 0.623, 0.727) and less turbulent (CI2 =1.77, 1.98, 2.31; R = 0, 1.6, 3.2). As in the case with a low value of α, increases in shock size cause an increase in the level of concentration and instability. This differs from the results with a low

Table 3.1 Statistics describing simulation results for stochastic positive feedback

	$\alpha = 0.002$, $\gamma = 0.1$	$\alpha = 0.02$, $\gamma = 0.1$	$\alpha = 0.2$, $\gamma = 0.1$	$\alpha = 0.002$, $\gamma = 0.2$	$\alpha = 0.02$, $\gamma = 0.2$	$\alpha = 0.2$, $\gamma = 0.2$
$\sigma = 0$						
HI1	0.29	0.526	0.248	0.4	0.382	0.42
HI2	1	0.926	0.298	0.489	0.49	0.48
II1	0.019	0.029	0.012	0.023	0.051	0.019
II2	0.002	0.002	0.002	0.002	0.002	0.002
CI1	1.32	1.86	1.2	1.51	1.45	1.55
CI2	2.51	2.4	1.37	1.7	1.73	1.69
R	0	0	0	0	0	1
n	1	1	4	2	2	1
TC	100	100	70	45	35	45
$\sigma = 0.05$						
HI1	0.47	0.45	0.36	0.565	0.438	0.508
HI2	0.98	0.82	0.46	0.97	0.514	0.66
II1	0.052	0.159	0.02	0.055	0.017	0.272
II2	0.002	0.002	0.002	0.002	0.002	0.002
CI1	1.76	1.5	1.36	1.76	1.56	1.13
CI2	2.48	2.08	1.6	2.3	1.77	1.93
R	2.3	1.5	1	1	0	1
n	1	1.3	2.5	1	2.3	2
TC	63	70	55	44	45	59.6
$\sigma = 0.1$						
HI1	0.62	0.66	0.33	0.96	0.503	0.538
HI2	0.86	0.84	0.44	0.976	0.623	0.628
II1	0.014	0.022	0.03	0.058	0.021	0.039
II2	0.002	0.002	0.002	0.002	0.002	0.002
CI1	3.2	2.13	1.36	1.83	1.75	1.62
CI2	4.04	2.37	1.61	2.94	1.98	1.79
R	5.3	5	3.2	3	1.6	1
n	1.3	1.3	3.2	2	2	2.5
TC	161	66	44	43.5	57.5	42.6
$\sigma = 0.2$						
HI1	0.88	0.57	0.426	0.565	0.557	0.429
HI2	0.87	0.90	0.53	0.97	0.727	0.725
II1	0.007	0.16	0.01	0.04	0.025	0.051
II2	0.002	0.002	0.002	0.002	0.002	0.002
CI1	2.56	2.02	1.5	2.5	2.03	2.05
CI2	2.6	2.04	1.6	3.3	2.31	2.65
R	3	4.7	2.6	4	3.2	3.5
n	1.3	1.25	2.6	1	1.5	1.75
TC	76	61	45	58	56.5	68

(a)   α = 0.2, γ = 0.1, no shock

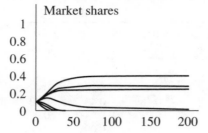

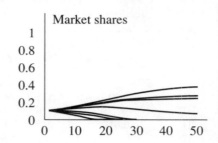

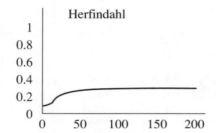

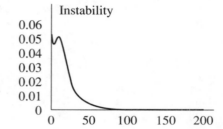

(b)   α = 0.2, γ = 0.1,   σ = 0.05

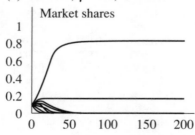

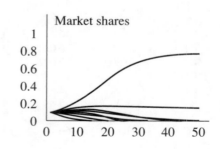

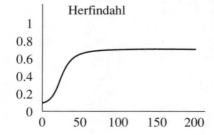

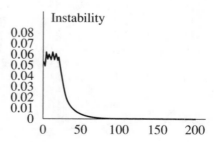

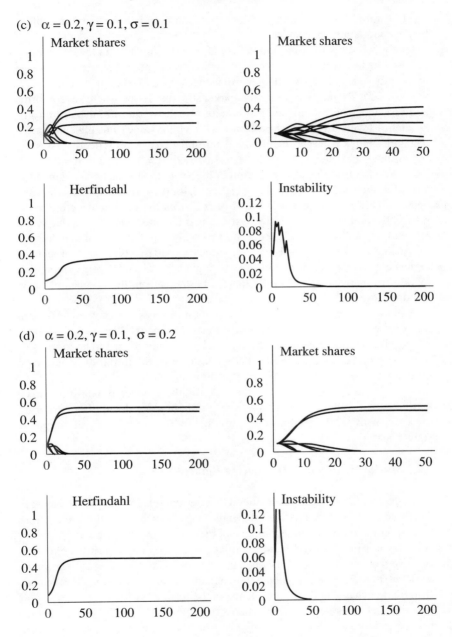

Figure 3.3   Stochastic increasing returns with α = 0.2, γ = 0.1 and different σ

level of initial cost variance, in which concentration is lowest and instability highest with a mid-size shock.

Lastly, we study the case with a very high α (Figure 3.3). In the deterministic case, the fast average rate of cost reduction causes market shares to converge to a steady state before switching has time to take place (HI2 = 0.29, CI2 = 1.37, R = 0, n = 5). There, the asymptotic market structure is one where several firms co-exist and where firm ranking is determined by the initial hierarchy of efficiency levels. In the stochastic case with a high value of α, the cumulative instability index is larger than in the deterministic case yet it decreases as the size of the shock increases (CI2 = 1.6, 1.61, 1.6; R = 1, 3.2, 2.6, n = 2.5, 3.2, 2.6). We also find that concentration is higher with stochastic shocks and is largest in the case of a large shock (HI2 = 0.46, 0.44, 0.53). Hence while the deterministic case with a high level of α causes the market structure to be relatively competitive, in the stochastic case it is more concentrated due to the effect of instability on the shakeout of firms. This might imply that in industries in which all firms' costs fall relatively quickly (due to a high level of technological opportunity) idiosyncratic events might prevent a relatively competitive market from emerging, as would instead be the case in the absence of those 'random' events.

A higher variance in the initial distribution of costs causes the Herfindahl index to be larger than in the case of the lower variance (HI2 = 0.46, 0.44, 0.53 versus HI2 = 0.660, 0.628, 0.725) and the level of turbulence to be lower. For any given level of α, the higher is the variance of the initial distribution of costs (γ), the more turbulence and concentration emerges.

We document the summary statistics for the case of dynamic positive feedback in Table 3.1 and interpret the results in more detail after exploring the case of dynamic decreasing returns below (see definitions of summary statistics above).

4.2   Stochastic Dynamic *Decreasing* Returns to Scale

In the deterministic model it was found that the market structure which emerges from dynamic *negative feedback* depends on the industry-specific average rate of cost reduction (α) and the variance of the initial cost distribution (γ). When α is very low or very high, results similar to the case of deterministic dynamic *positive* feedback emerge. It is when average costs are falling at an *intermediate* level, that the richness embodied in dynamic negative feedback is revealed; firm market shares undergo turbulence in the form of switching since as soon as a firm becomes large, its rate of cost reduction falls, and it is surpassed by a faster-growing small firm. For any given level of α, the higher is the variance of the initial distribution of costs (γ), the more turbulent and concentrated is the emergent market structure.

We start as usual with a low industry average rate of cost reduction and recall that in the deterministic case, when α is very low there is no turbulence in market shares; inertia overwhelms the dynamic and only the initially most fit firm survives. Figure 3.4 displays results with a relatively low speed of cost adjustment ($\alpha = 0.002$), and a relatively low variance of the initial cost distribution ($\gamma = 0.1$). The dynamics illustrated in Figure 3.4 indicate that, as in the case of stochastic dynamic *positive* feedback, the addition of a stochastic component to costs does not alter the emergence of concentration, it alters the *path* towards concentration and the final ranking of firms. However, unlike the deterministic case where turbulence and switching occur only with a mid-level value of α, switching here emerges even with a low α, and although concentration always results due to the effect of selection on inertia, the final leader is not (necessarily) the initially most efficient firm. This result was also found with a low level of α in the case of stochastic positive feedback.

The effect of different size shocks can be seen clearly in Table 3.2, below. As the shock increases in size, the final Herfindahl index decreases (HI2 = 0.98, 0.892, 0.77) and the number of surviving firms increases (n = 1, 1.2, 1.6). A larger shock also makes the cumulative instability index rise (CI2 = 2.76, 4.08, 6.35) and the number of changes in rank rise (R = 3, 5, 6.2). Larger shocks thus make the market more *competitive* on its way towards *monopoly*. Lastly, we note that with a given α and γ, increasing the size of the shock first makes the convergence time increase very much and then decrease (TC = 70, 157, 137). The convergence time is thus the longest with a mid-size shock. This is because a shock that is very large causes a strong shakeout of firms, while a shock that is not very large allows the selection mechanism to remain strong and hence one firm to dominate quickly; a mid-size shock has the effect of increasing the path of turbulence and hence delaying the time of convergence to a steady state.

As was also noted in the deterministic case, with a given value of α and σ, the larger is the variance in the initial distribution of costs (except in the case with large shocks), the more concentrated and more turbulent is the resulting market structure (HI2 = 0.953, 0.976, 0.98; CI2 = 2.9, 5.57, 2.63; R = 2, 6, 4.3).

Figure 3.5 illustrates the results with a mid-level value of α. We recall that in the deterministic negative feedback case, a mid-level value of α causes the market to experience turbulence in market shares; switching and general instability emerge due to the effect of alternating advantages between firms.

With the addition of a stochastic component to costs, instability is even stronger; shares do not only switch, as in the deterministic case, but also experience longer more frequent and jagged ups and downs. In Table 3.2, below we see that as shocks increase, concentration rises (HI2 = 0.39, 0.71, 0.731) while instability falls (CI2 = 4.6, 4.2, 4.58; R = 7, 5, 4.75). We also see that with a given value of α and γ, the larger is the shock the quicker market shares

(a)　α = 0.002, γ = 0.1, no shock

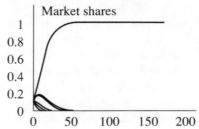

Market shares

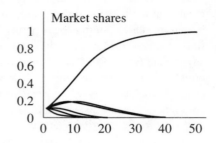

Market shares

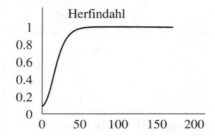

Herfindahl

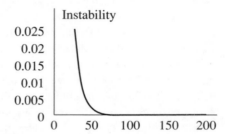

Instability

(b)　α = 0.002, γ = 0.1,　σ = 0.05

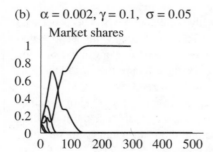

Market shares

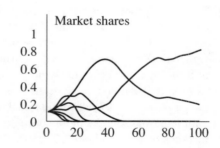

Market shares

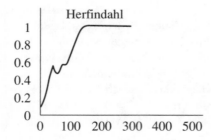

Herfindahl

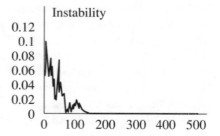

Instability

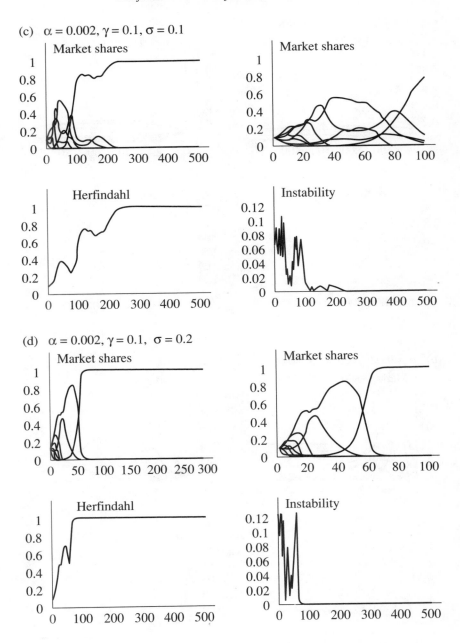

Figure 3.4 Stochastic decreasing returns with α = 0.002, γ = 0.1 and different σ

(a) $\alpha = 0.02$, $\gamma = 0.1$, no shock

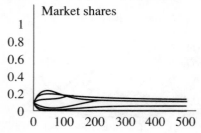

Market shares

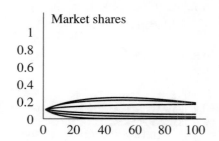

Market shares

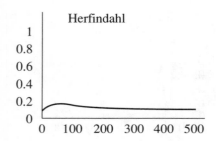

Herfindahl

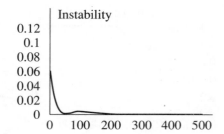

Instability

(b) $\alpha = 0.02$, $\gamma = 0.1$, $\sigma = 0.05$

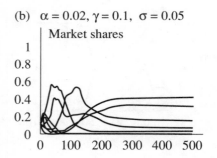

Market shares

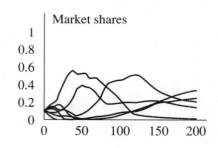

Market shares

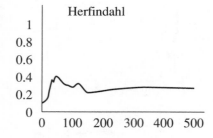

Herfindahl

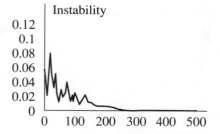

Instability

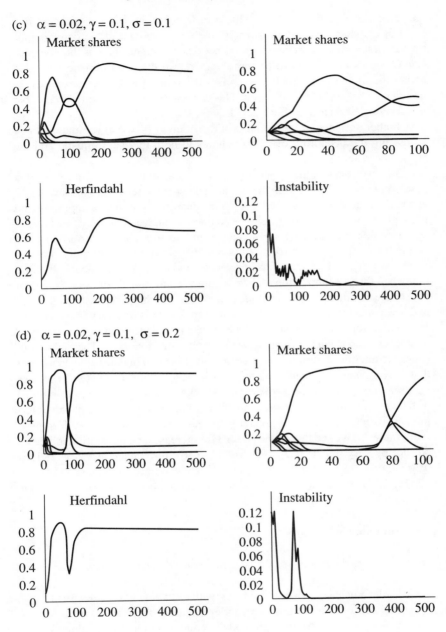

(c) $\alpha = 0.02, \gamma = 0.1, \sigma = 0.1$

(d) $\alpha = 0.02, \gamma = 0.1, \sigma = 0.2$

Figure 3.5 Stochastic decreasing returns with $\alpha = 0.02$, $\gamma = 0.1$ and different σ

converge (TC = 296, 182, 166). This is different from the case of a very low level of α, where instead an increase in shock size caused the convergence time to first increase and then to decrease. The difference here is that the mid-size α causes the market to be turbulent even in the deterministic case, and hence the increase in shock size causes the market to become excessively turbulent, 'shaking' many firms out. This can also be noted by the fall in number of surviving firms as the shock gets larger (n = 3.6, 2.6, 2.25).

A higher variance in the initial cost distribution ($\gamma = 0.2$) has the effect of increasing the instability of market shares in both the deterministic and the stochastic case.

Lastly, we consider the case with a very fast rate of cost reduction. Since this case is not very different from that found with positive feedback, we save space and review the results only verbally. In the deterministic case, a high α caused the asymptotic market structure to be characterized by a relatively low level of concentration and no switching or changes in rank to occur. This was due to the fact that the effect of convergence (caused by costs falling very quickly for all firms) outweighed both the effect of selection and of negative feedback. We find that when the fast innovation regime is subjected to shocks, the shocks are not able to greatly alter the deterministic pattern; no switching, survival of all firms, and low concentration. This is different from the cases of a very low and mid-level value for α where instead shocks cause turbulence and changes in rank to emerge even when the final market structure is a monopoly. The inability of shocks to alter the deterministic pattern in the case of a high α is due to the fact that convergence dominates both the process of selection and the two processes creating variety (negative feedback and shocks). Although this was also noted in the case of stochastic positive feedback, the impenetrability of the deterministic case with a high α is greater in the case of dynamic *negative* feedback.

In Table 3.2 we see that as the shock size increases, concentration increases but not by very much (HI2 = 0.1, 0.127, 0.16); turbulence increases (CI2 = 0.307, 0.604, 0.822; R = 0, 2.3, 2); and the convergence time increases (TC = 19, 23, 27.3). These same relationships emerge with a higher variance of the initial cost distribution ($\gamma = 0.1$).

4.3   Summary of Results

We summarize the results for the case of stochastic feedback below:

- Under stochastic positive feedback with *any* value of α (industry average rate of cost reduction), and under negative feedback with a *low* α, although concentration still tends to emerge (in the former due to path-dependency and in the latter due to inertia), the *process* towards concentration is very different; turbulence precedes concentration, and the

Table 3.2 *Statistics describing simulation results for stochastic negative feedback*

	$\alpha = 0.002,$ $\gamma = 0.1$	$\alpha = 0.02,$ $\gamma = 0.1$	$\alpha = 0.2,$ $\gamma = 0.1$	$\alpha = 0.002,$ $\gamma = 0.2$	$\alpha = 0.02,$ $\gamma = 0.2$	$\alpha = 0.2,$ $\gamma = 0.2$
$\sigma = 0$						
HI1	0.74	0.16	0.1	0.399	0.313	0.16
HI2	0.97	0.134	0.1	0.483	0.134	0.134
II1	0.02	0.004	0.001	0.022	0.004	0.004
II2	0.002	0.002	0.002	0.002	0.002	0.002
CI1	1.8	0.994	0.235	1.49	0.994	0.994
CI2	2.1	1.29	0.236	1.69	1.29	1.29
R	0	4	0	0	4	4
n	1	10	10	2	10	10
TC	50	200	15	45	200	200
$\sigma = 0.05$						
HI1	0.33	0.58	0.105	0.608	0.53	0.133
HI2	0.98	0.39	0.1	0.953	0.396	0.141
II1	0.052	0.004	0.01	0.03	0.016	0.018
II2	0.002	0.002	0.002	0.002	0.002	0.002
CI1	1.66	3.6	0.244	2	4.25	0.518
CI2	2.76	4.6	0.307	2.9	5.21	0.586
R	3	7	0	2	0.7	1.3
n	1	3.6	10	1	4	10
TC	70	296	19	66	306	20
$\sigma = 0.1$						
HI1	0.698	0.69	0.119	0.626	0.691	0.128
HI2	0.892	0.71	0.127	0.976	0.556	0.13
II1	0.016	0.006	0.021	0.04	0.007	0.02
II2	0.002	0.002	0.002	0.002	0.002	0.002
CI1	3.24	2.68	0.496	4.07	2.92	0.513
CI2	4.08	4.2	0.604	5.57	4.31	0.598
R	5	5	2.3	6	6.25	1
n	1.2	2.6	10	1	3.25	10
TC	157	182	23	186	226	20
$\sigma = 0.2$						
HI1	0.506	0.76	0.14	0.726	0.602	0.138
HI2	0.77	0.731	0.16	0.98	0.7	0.131
II1	0.018	0.008	0.021	0.035	0.029	0.026
II2	0.002	0.002	0.002	0.002	0.002	0.002
CI1	5.24	3.54	0.698	2.32	2.55	0.656
CI2	6.35	4.58	0.822	2.63	3.26	0.762
R	6.2	4.75	2	4.3	3.6	2.66
n	1.6	2.25	10	1	2	10
TC	137	166	27.3	57	130	23.3

concentration is very different; turbulence precedes concentration, and the final leader is not necessarily the initially most efficient firm.

- The presence of shocks always renders unpredictable which firms will finally lead the industry: information regarding initial efficiency levels does not provide information on final ranking.
- When α is very high, the deterministic results are less affected by the presence of shocks. This is due to the fact that when the industry average rate of cost reduction is high, convergence dominates both the process of selection as well as the negative/positive feedback process creating variety between firms. This result is even stronger in the case of negative feedback. This implies that in industries in which the average rate of cost reduction is very high, idiosyncratic events have less of an impact on industry evolution. The stochastic case with a high α produces a less competitive market structure than the deterministic case with a high α. *This implies that in industries with a fast average rate of cost reduction, the occurrence of shocks (idiosyncratic events) might produce a less competitive market structure than the case in absence of those 'events'.*
- Market share instability is greatest with *mid*-size shocks since small shocks are not very 'disturbing' and large shocks cause too large a shakeout and hence early concentration. In the stochastic negative feedback case with a mid-level speed of cost reduction parameter, instability is higher than in the deterministic case; shares not only undergo changes in rank and switching but also experience longer more frequent and jagged ups and downs. *Emphasis should thus not be placed only on large radical events affecting change but also and especially on minor events.*
- In the case of stochastic negative feedback with a low α, although the market tends to become concentrated (as in the deterministic case), as the shock size increases, the degree of concentration decreases and the instability index rises. Larger shocks thus make the market more competitive on its way to monopoly.
- In the case of stochastic dynamic positive feedback, a higher variance of the initial cost distribution, causes the level of instability to be lower than with a lower variance. This might be because the higher degree of initial differences between firms makes the market structure less vulnerable to shocks due to the stronger force of selection.
- In both types of feedback, when costs change very slowly convergence to stability (instability index $= 0.002$) takes the longest time to occur with a mid-size shock. This is because large shocks cause many firms to exit, while small shocks cause the selection mechanism to remain strong. The mid-size shock has the effect of increasing turbulence and hence delaying the time of convergence to a steady state. This result does not hold under

decreasing returns with a mid-level α, where instead an increase in shock size causes the convergence time to first increase and then to decrease. This is because the mid-size α under negative feedback causes the market to be turbulent even without a shock, hence the increase in shock size causes the market to become excessively turbulent.

5   CONCLUSION

The stochastic analysis allows us to understand better the particular role of randomness in industry evolution. A deterministic and a stochastic version of the model were developed separately so that the interaction between structural and random factors could be explored. In contrast to studies which make all underlying dynamics based on stochastic shocks (for example, firm growth modeled as a Gibrat process), economic change occurs in the model due to the interaction between initial conditions, shocks and the underlying non-linear structural dynamics related to firm size.

The patterns that emerge from the stochastic model shed light on Klepper's (1996) hypothesis that market share turbulence during the early phase of the industry life-cycle, and/or in certain types of industries, might be the result of idiosyncratic (random) events which disrupt the path-dependent effects of selection under positive feedback:

> The result (of increasing returns) is a world in which initial firm differences get magnified as size begets size … The starkness of the model precludes any departures from this evolutionary pattern. This can be remedied by allowing for random events that alter the relative standing of incumbents and potential entrants. If cohorts differ in terms of the distribution of their innovative expertise or if the innovative expertise of incumbents is undermined by certain types of technological changes, then later entrants may leapfrog over the industry leaders and the firms that eventually dominate the industry may not come from the earliest cohort of entrants. (Klepper, 1996, p. 581)

We explored the *degree* to which shocks affect the path-dependent pattern under different types of conditions. The industry-specific conditions included the type of feedback regulating the relationship between firm size and innovation, the average rate of cost reduction in the industry (or technological opportunity), and the different level of initial asymmetry between firms.

The *deterministic* analysis indicates that when small firms are favored in the process of innovation (dynamic negative feedback), the market structure tends to be more unstable (with switching in firm ranking) and less concentrated. When instead it is larger firms that have the innovative advantage (dynamic positive feedback), the emergent market structure tends to be more concentrated and stable (concentration emerges without any switching in firm market shares). The exact patterns are determined by the industry-specific speed of cost reduction parameter (α) as well as by the parameter describing the initial variance between firm efficiencies (γ).

In the *stochastic* version of the model, new results emerge. Under positive feedback, and under negative feedback with a very low speed of cost-reduction parameter, although concentration still tends to emerge, the *process* towards concentration is very different from the deterministic case. Market share switching and general instability precedes concentration, so that observers only interested in the asymptotic level of concentration risk missing important qualitative information regarding industry evolution. That is, *to understand market evolution fully, one should look not only at the level of concentration at one point in time, but also at the process of instability and concentration which leads up to that state*. The stochastic model illustrated that the empirical regularities can be reproduced by those life-cycle studies which emphasize the effect of idiosyncratic events on positive feedback (Klepper and Graddy, 1990; Klepper, 1996; Arthur, 1990).

It was found that when the speed of cost adjustment parameter is very high, the deterministic results are less affected by the presence of shocks. This implies that in industries in which the rate of diffusion is very high (for example in industries with a 'codifiable' knowledge base), idiosyncratic events have less of an effect on industry evolution. In both types of feedback, turbulence (as measured by the instability index and the rank index) was found to be the highest with *mid*-size shocks since small shocks are not very 'disturbing' and large shocks cause too large of a shakeout and hence early concentration. In the stochastic negative feedback case with a mid-level speed of cost reduction parameter, instability was higher than in the deterministic case: shares not only undergo changes in rank and switching but also experience longer, more frequent and jagged ups and downs. Emphasis should thus not be placed only on large radical events affecting change but also and especially on minor events.

NOTE

1. The quotation by Tjalling Koopmans (Koopmans, 1937) is used here since he and his contemporaries, Wesley Mitchell and Henry Moore, initiated the discussion on the use of stochastic concepts in neoclassical economics. The quotation and an excellent summary of the debate is found in Mirowski (1989, p. 235).

4. Market share instability and stock price volatility during the industry life-cycle: the US automobile industry[*]

1 INTRODUCTION

As discussed in Chapters 1 and 2, market share instability, during certain stages of an industry's life-cycle, has become a 'stylized fact' in the industrial organization literature. This has caused new indices of competition and new ideas regarding firm size distributions to emerge (Gort, 1963; Hymer and Pashigian, 1962; Ijiri and Simon, 1977). In the finance literature, volatility in the form of *excess volatility*, that is, the much larger volatility of stock prices than dividends (although stock prices theoretically trace the present value of future dividends), has given rise to new ideas regarding stock price determination (Campbell and Shiller, 1988; Shiller, 1989). Both fields have gone through a similar set of reactions to the phenomenon of volatility, divided between those who try to interpret it with traditional theory and those who instead go to the opposite extreme, offering quasi-non-economic explanations. An example of the latter is the use of stochastic processes (for example, Gibrat's Law) to reproduce firm-size distributions, and the claim by Shiller (1989) that stock price volatility has more to do with investors' 'over-reactions' (due to herd effects and fashions) than with strict movements in fundamentals.

Recent evolutionary models, both theoretical and empirical, have tied the presence of market share instability to industry-specific variables. Empirical studies have found market share instability to be higher during the *early* stage of an industry's life-cycle (Klepper, 1996), in industries in which *small* firms are more innovative (Acs and Audretsch, 1990), and in industries characterized as 'Schumpeter *Mark I*', that is, industries with high entry, less persistence in firms' ability to innovate, and a more codifiable knowledge base (Malerba and Orsenigo, 1996). Evolutionary simulation models by Dosi et al. (1995) and Mazzucato (1998), which connect the emergence of different industrial structures to alternative types of 'technological regimes', both find that the Mark I regime is characterized by more market share instability.

The object of our study is to explore whether there is a relationship between market share instability and stock price volatility and to what degree this relationship is connected with the concept of the industry life-cycle. Since neither life-cycle studies nor finance studies have studied the relationship between these two forms of market turbulence, we use insights from both fields to develop hypotheses concerning the possible relationship. We then compare such hypotheses to the empirical patterns in one particular industry, the US automobile industry, for which detailed data regarding market shares, earnings and stock prices can be collected for most of its history. This is a particularly interesting industry to look at because of the many, sometimes contrasting, studies that have connected the evolution of its market structure (number of firms, instability, concentration) to underlying changes in competition, innovation and production. Given the industry-specific nature of market share instability, an empirical relationship between market share instability and excess volatility could suggest that while over-reaction explains the *existence* of excess volatility, industry-specific factors contribute to the *degree* of excess volatility.

The relationship between changes in market shares and changes in stock prices is particularly relevant to an evolutionary perspective since such changes represent two different types of *selection* mechanisms, one at the product market level and the other at the stock market level. Models in evolutionary economics often make a firm's market share a function of its relative fitness condition and formalize this 'distance from mean' dynamic using replicator equations (Silverberg et al., 1988; Metcalfe, 1994). Stock prices, however, are less affected by current fitness than by *expected* future fitness. Hence in periods of high market share instability, during which there is less predictability of future firm growth patterns, it may be that a 10 per cent increase in a firm's market share sends a very different signal to the stock market than the same 10 per cent increase during a more stable period. The study considers these types of issues when developing hypotheses on the relationship between market share instability and stock market volatility.

The chapter is organized as follows. Section 2 reviews the stylized facts regarding market share instability and stock price volatility in the US automobile industry and some associated measurement issues. The patterns observed here are decreasing market share instability as the industry gets older, a rising degree of market concentration, and the presence of excess volatility of stock prices. Section 3 contains some background history of the US automobile industry regarding changes in innovation, market shares and demand. Section 4 reviews some possible explanations of the empirical regularities using ideas from life-cycle theories and from finance theory. Insights and implications from both approaches are used to develop hypotheses concerning the relationship between market share instability and excess volatility. Section 5 reports statistical results obtained from data on market shares, earnings and stock prices for the US automobile industry from 1921 to 1995. Both the firm- and industry-level data are divided into sub-periods in order to evaluate whether there are distinct patterns of volatility in different phases of industry evolution.

2   STYLIZED FACTS REGARDING STOCK PRICE VOLATILITY

Before considering the possible relationship between market share instability and stock price volatility, we review the actual patterns, volatility measurement issues and some traditional explanations. Having already described the theoretical and measurement issues regarding market share instability in Chapters 2 and 3, we concentrate here on stock price volatility.

Although stock prices should, according to the Efficient Market Theory (EMM), represent the present value of future dividends (for example, the efficient discounting of new information), the actual variability in stock prices has been found to be much larger than that of fundamentals, causing many to question the validity of the theory. Shiller (1989) formalizes the concept of 'excess volatility' through the analysis of variance inequalities. The EMM states that the real price is the expectation of discounted future dividends:

$$v_t = E_t v^*_t \tag{4.1}$$

$$v^*_t = \sum_{k=0}^{\infty} D_{t+k} \prod_{j=0}^{k} \gamma_{t+j} \tag{4.2}$$

where v^*_t is the *ex-post* rational or perfect-foresight price, D_{t+k} is the dividend stream, γ_{t+j} is a real discount factor equal to $1/(1 + r_{t+j})$, and r_{t+j} is the short (one-period) rate of discount at time $t + j$. If equation (4.2) holds, and if we assume for simplicity a constant discount rate r, then since $v^*_t = v_t + u_t$ (where u_t is the error term), it can be shown that there is an *upper bound* to the variability of stock prices given by:

$$\sigma\left(\Delta v^*_t\right) \leq \sigma(D_t)/\sqrt{2r} \tag{4.3}$$

where σ denotes standard deviation (for formal proof, see Shiller, 1989, p. 82). That is, the EMM predicts not only that changes in stock prices should reflect innovations in discounted dividends but also that the volatility of dividends (fundamentals) should be larger than the volatility of stock prices. The data instead show that it is exactly the opposite: stock prices are much more volatile than discounted dividends, causing many to question whether they reflect movements in dividends at all.[1]

The concept of excess volatility can be illustrated graphically by manipulating stock price and dividend data as Shiller (1989) did for the S&P 500. The stock price and dividend time-series data are first divided by the Consumer Price Index and then de-trended using an exponential trend line to make sure that the series are stationary and hence their variances comparable. To calculate the series (v_t) generated by the EMM the following equation is used recursively:

$$v_t = \frac{v_{t+1} + D_t}{(1+r)} \tag{4.4}$$

where r is the constant discount rate and D the dividend per share.[2] The calculations can also be made based on earnings/share since studies have shown this not to affect the result of excess volatility (Shiller, 1989). Given the lag in equation (4.4), it is not possible to calculate the EMM for the last period. If there are 100 periods, the value for the EMM at $t = 99$ is calculated by using the actual stock price at $t = 100$ in place of v_{t+1} in equation (4.4). Then for each other value from $t = 1$ to $t = 98$, equation (4.4) is used. In Figure 4.1, we document the results that emerge from this procedure for three sets of data: the S&P 500 index data (the data used by Shiller, 1989), the aggregate US automobile data, and the data for one particular firm, General Motors. The per share stock price and dividend data for the S&P 500 and for the automobile industry are taken from *Standard & Poor's Analyst Handbook*, while that for General Motors is taken from the annual editions (1924–97) of *Moody's Manual of Investments*. To adjust for the effect of macroeconomic factors, the industry level and firm level data are divided by the corresponding S&P 500 data. Since average dividend data for the automobile industry are available only from 1946 onwards, in Figure 4.1 we illustrate the EMM price from 1946 to 1995. The stock price and dividend data for General Motors have been adjusted for stock splits with information on splits obtained from *Moody's*. In each of the three cases, we observe excess volatility: the line tracing the actual de-trended stock price is much more volatile than the line tracing the EMM.

The sections below will not study the *origin* of excess volatility in the automobile industry, but rather the forces that contribute to the *degree* of excess volatility over time.

3   BRIEF HISTORICAL BACKGROUND OF THE US AUTOMOBILE INDUSTRY

The US automobile industry began around 1894 with a total of four producers in the industry. By 1909 that number had reached 275! (See Figure 4.2). This

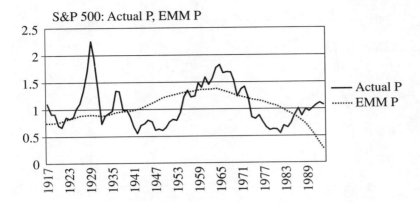

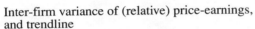

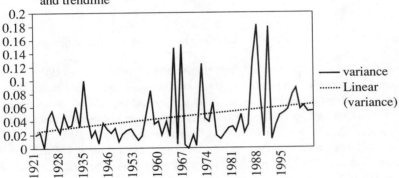

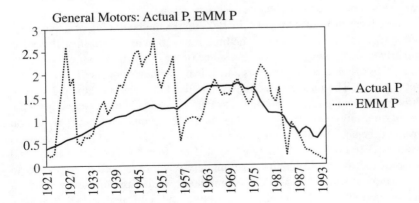

Figure 4.1   Excess volatility

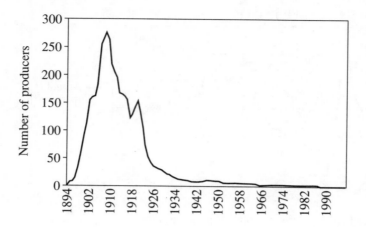

Source: *Ward's Automotive Yearbook.*

Figure 4.2   Number of car producers in the US automobile industry

first stage, which approximately covers the period from 1894 to 1909, was a pioneering one in which product design was not standardized and demand was not stable. Many different designs, technologies and propulsion systems were tried. The trial-and-error stage led to much oscillation in market shares. In his ranking of the 28 most successful cars produced between 1903 and 1924, Epstein (1928) describes the large instability in market shares which made market shares in 1903 bad predictors of market shares in the 1920s: of the ten leaders in 1924, only three were in business prior to 1908. On the consumer side, cars were more of a hobby than a necessity.

The advent of Ford's Model T in 1909 marks the beginning of a new stage in the US automobile industry. The high innovation and flexibility of Ford in its early years allowed it to take advantage of the opportunity which the 1910s and 1920s offered: rising incomes and a rising demand for cars (as necessities, not hobbies). The mass production system used to make the Model T caused throughput time to fall from 21 days to four days and cut labor hours by 60 per cent (Abernathy and Wayne, 1974). In 1909, when Ford's cost reduction program began, it had a market share of only 10 per cent (GM 23 per cent) while in 1916 Ford had 40 per cent and in 1921 almost 60 per cent. This second stage of the industry, which approximately covers the period from 1909 to 1927, during which the Model T dominated production and sales, marks a distinct period. The new standardized product and stable demand allowed Ford to reap large economies of scale and remain the market leader for two decades. Economies of scale contributed to the strong shakeout (of smaller producers) which occurred in the beginning of the period: by 1930 there were only a dozen firms left. Figure 4.2 illustrates that the steady decline in the number of automobile producers (the beginning of the 'shakeout') started to occur precisely in the year that the Model T was introduced.

A third stage, covering the period from 1927 to 1940, marks the great change in market shares which occurred when Ford lost its first place position to General Motors (GM). As has already been discussed in Chapter 2, and as will be seen again in Section 4, below, some economists have attributed this fall to Ford's large size and concentration on mass production which prevented it from (flexibly) foreseeing the changing nature of demand. GM quickly responded to the new demand for a heavier closed body and more comfortable car, while Ford was overcome with inertia. Others have attributed Ford's loss of leadership to the idiosyncratic nature of Henry Ford's personality. Nevertheless, from 1926 to 1940, GM increased its market share from 20 to 50 per cent while Ford fell from 50 to 20 per cent. After this time, GM never lost its lead among US producers. Market shares became much more *predictable* than in the period from 1900 to 1930.

In the 1950s small cars began to enter the US market, but only with the energy crisis of the 1970s did foreign imports of small cars seriously affect US producers' market shares. The market shares of US producers (as a percentage of US production only) since the 1970s have not changed much, with most of the changes occurring between US and foreign-made cars.

4   THEORETICAL INSIGHTS: LIFE-CYCLE AND FINANCE THEORY

Having reviewed in Section 2 the way that the characteristic patterns of market share instability and stock price volatility apply to the US automobile industry, and in Section 3 the underlying historical events in that industry, we now ask how the volatility in market shares and stock prices might be related to each other.

To do so, we first review different life-cycle perspectives on market share instability. We then ask what implications these perspectives may have for the evolution of stock price volatility. We are interested in life-cycle analysis because of its emphasis on how industry patterns *evolve* over time. Since there is no life-cycle literature which explicitly connects market share instability and stock price volatility, we turn to some ideas in finance theory regarding uncertainty and stock price determination to provide more insight on the possible connection. At the end of this section, some informal hypotheses are drawn based on insights from both the life-cycle and finance literature. These hypotheses are used to interpret the data in Section 5.

4.1   Market Share Instability: Life-cycle and Technological Regimes

The industry life-cycle literature, as well as the Schumpeterian literature on technological regimes, has drawn links between industry evolution and market share instability. Gort and Klepper (1982) found the following stylized facts to hold across 46 products: during the early stage of an industry's evolution, there is high entry with many small firms and the product price is relatively high. This phase is characterized by market share instability and relatively low concentration. As entry and total output increase, the product price falls. At some point, the number of producers reaches a peak, after which it falls steadily (a 'shakeout'), although total industry output continues to rise. This stage is characterized by more market share stability and greater market concentration.

Life-cycle models have attempted to provide explanations, both formal and informal, of the dynamics underlying the above regularities. We reviewed two different life-cycle models in Chapter 3, Section 2. We saw that one group of life-cycle theories claims that changes in market share patterns result from a 'switch' in regime from negative feedback between size and innovation to positive feedback (Abernathy and Wayne, 1974; Klein, 1977). In this view, the strong economies of scale in the US automobile industry from 1909 to 1924 resulted in market share stability, while the changing nature of demand at the end of the 1920s (which required more flexible and explorative strategies to be used) led to more market share instability. When demand and technology became stable again, so did market shares.

This point made in this first set of life-cycle theories is similar to that made by recent contributions in the Schumpeterian literature connecting market structure and technological regimes (Malerba and Orsenigo, 1996). The technological regime called Schumpeter Mark I refers to those industries, or periods during the industry life-cycle, which are characterized by high rates of entry, less persistence in firms' abilities to innovate, and a more codifiable knowledge base. Under these conditions of 'creative destruction', it is more common for innovators to be small firms. Mark II is instead characterized by strong economies of scale, more persistence in innovation, and a tacit knowledge base, causing a 'success breeds success' dynamic. Under these conditions it is more common to find that typical innovators are large firms. The distinction between Mark I and Mark II can take place both between different periods in an industry's life-cycle (the early period is characterized more by Mark I while the mature period by Mark II), as well as between different industries or sectors. For example, Malerba and Orsenigo (1996) find that the chemical sector falls more into Mark II while the mechanical engineering sector falls more into

Mark I. Likewise, the shampoo industry is characterized more by Mark I but automobiles by Mark II. Empirical studies by Malerba and Orsenigo (1996) have found market share instability to be higher in Mark I industries and concentration to be higher in Mark II industries. In an evolutionary simulation model which explores the types of market structures which emerge from these different types of technological regimes, Dosi et al. (1995) find that the former are characterized by more market share instability than the latter. Similarly, in the simulation model described in Chapter 2 (Mazzucato, 1998), in which Mark I (II) is defined as the negative (positive) effect of size on the rate of cost reduction, market share instability is also found to be more characteristic of the Mark I period.

Another set of life-cycle theories include those reviewed in Chapter 3 by Klepper and Graddy (1990) and Klepper (1996). In this view, it is not 'switches' in regime that cause different types of market instability and concentration to emerge. Instead, there is always *positive* feedback between size and innovation, but this does not lead to a monotonic increase in concentration because of the effect of randomly distributed innovation capabilities and timing of entry, which cause the early stage of the industry to be characterized by more market share instability. Market share instability later declines as a few firms get ahead and price–cost margins fall, reducing firm incentives to grow given the related costs of adjustment. Similarly to the work of Arthur (1990), the role of chance events in the early evolution of the industry is emphasized: '... small fortuitous events – unexpected orders, chance meetings with buyers, managerial whims – to determine which ones achieve early sales and, over time, which firms dominate' (Arthur, 1994, p. 5).

Having reviewed the way that Schumpeterian and life-cycle theorists have connected market share instability to industry-specific factors, we now review some ideas in finance theory to gain insight into the possible co-evolution of market share instability and stock price volatility.

4.2 Stock Price Volatility: Insights from Finance Theory

How might the market share patterns described above affect stock price changes? Basing their work on the stylized facts found in Gort and Klepper (1982), Jovanovic and MacDonald (1994b) make some predictions concerning the evolution of the average industry stock price around the shakeout period of the industry life-cycle. Focussing on the US tire industry, they build a model which assumes that an industry is born as a result of a basic invention and that the shakeout occurs as a result of one major refinement to that invention.[3] They predict that just before the shakeout occurs the average stock price will fall because the new innovation precipitates a fall in product price which is bad news for incumbents. Later, as some firms establish themselves as early winners in the innovation race, the index rises sharply, reflecting those firms' enormous increase in both market share and value. Finally the index declines as the innovation diffuses, dissipating the rents earned by early innovators. (Jovanovic and MacDonald, 1994b, pp. 344–5)

Although Jovanovic and MacDonald (1994b) is one of the few papers which directly connects the industry life-cycle to the evolution of stock prices, it does so at the industry level (and only during one specific period of the life-cycle), so that inter-firm variations are not accounted for, and it is only the *level* of stock prices, not stock price *volatility* over time, that is the focus. Our analysis adds to both of these dimensions.

Indeed, the possible co-evolution of market share instability and stock price volatility is rooted in the mechanism by which market share instability affects 'uncertainty' and how uncertainty affects stock prices. Market share instability creates the type of 'uncertainty' which Frank Knight distinguished from 'risk':

> The practical difference between the two categories, risk and uncertainty, is that in the former the distribution of the outcome in a group of instances is known (either from calculation a priori or from statistics of past experience). While in the case of uncertainty that is not true, the reason being in general that it is impossible to form a group of instances, because the situation dealt with is in a high degree unique ... (Knight, 1964, pp. 232–3, quoted in Shiller, 1989, p. 13)

It is 'uncertainty' which Klein (1977) describes when reporting the market share instability in the early phase of the US auto industry's life-cycle which made market shares in the 1930s completely unpredictable based on market shares in the early 1900s. What is the impact of the uncertainty arising from market share instability on the speculative evaluation of firms? One might postulate that in periods of higher market share instability (for example, Mark I), investors are less willing to use current market share as a signal of future performance and hence base the firm's market value less on its market share. This would suggest a period in which there is less correlation between a firm's market share and its stock price. At the same time, there may be more excess volatility during this period because of the constant corrections which investors must make to their previous predictions. We consider such hypotheses below after reviewing some basic concepts in finance theory.

In standard finance models, the stock price is taken to be the present value of future dividends or earnings. Letting P stand for the price of a share, D the (annual) dividend per share in the previous year, r the appropriate rate of discount, and g the expected growth in dividends, we have (provided $g < r$, otherwise the price is infinite):

$$P = \sum_{i=1}^{\infty} D \frac{(1+g)^i}{(1+r)^i}. \qquad (4.5)$$

In equation (4.5), both r and g could be made time-varying. The same equation can be expressed in terms of the price–earnings ratio. Dividing each side by earnings per share, E, and summing, we obtain an expression for the price–earnings ratio:

$$\frac{P}{E} = \frac{D}{E} \frac{(1+g)}{(r-g)}. \qquad (4.6)$$

The price–earnings ratio is thus a function of the dividend payout ratio and the expected long-term growth rate of the dividend stream (both equations are developed in Malkiel and Cragg, 1970).[4]

Under uncertainty it is the *expected* dividends or earnings (and their future growth rate) that are relevant. The presence of *risk* can be incorporated into equation (4.6) with a term representing the (expected) variance of the future returns stream from each stock. Since the horizon over which growth can be forecasted is a function of the variability of returns (the higher variance causes less predictability), the *P/E* should be negatively related to the variance term (Malkiel and Cragg, 1970).[5] An important measure of risk called the Beta index, used in the context of the EMM (or CAPM) model, looks at the covariance between the returns of each individual security and that of a composite market index (the higher the covariance, the higher the risk). Covariances are assumed to emerge due to the fact that all individual (firm) returns partially depend on the returns in the whole market (such as the S&P index), or on the returns of a particular industry (Beaver and Morse, 1978). *Ceteris paribus*, a stock whose movements are not highly correlated with the market (a low Beta) will tend to reduce the variability and hence also reduce the risk of the portfolio, causing the price–earnings of the stock to increase (Malkiel and Cragg, 1970). Yet the fact that the covariances and variances that are being valued in the market are those *perceived* by investors, not some 'true' set, means that this relationship is not so predictable. For example, a higher dividend payout should theoretically, in equation (4.2), cause the *P/E* to increase, yet if the high dividend payout is interpreted to mean low future growth (due to low reinvested earnings), then it could actually cause the *P/E* to fall.

Shiller's (1989) theoretical and empirical studies have contributed to this analysis of market evaluation by emphasizing the role of 'social' factors. He has shown that the efficient markets hypothesis faces serious problems due to the much larger volatility of stock prices than dividends. He has suggested that the reason for this 'over-reaction' might lie in the way that investors interact with each other and the degree to which popular models (driven by factors like: intuition, the diffusion of opinions, herd effects, and social movements) affect expectations about the future and investment behavior.

We ask how all the above factors, that is, dividend payouts, the expected growth of earnings, the expected risk, and the social psychology of investors, might be related to market share instability, and to the processes underlying such patterns discussed in the life-cycle theories in Section 4.1, above. The connection can be posited principally through the effect of market share instability on investors' abilities to forecast market values.

As regards the effect of market share instability on investors' anticipation of firm *growth*, various studies, including Ryals (1985) and Beaver and Morse (1978), have found that the *P/E* ratio is strongly affected by investors' attitudes, confidence and moods (Keynesian 'animal spirits'). Beaver and Morse (1978) have attempted to measure the emotional anticipation of future events with detailed data reflecting how security companies make their predictions. They find growth anticipations to have less to do with the statistical patterns of *past* growth (the traditional way that economists have incorporated anticipated growth into models) than with more subtle ways in which expectations are formed.[6] Thus in a period of high market share instability, since investors have less information regarding firm growth prospects, they might be less 'confident' to give a high price to a firm which experiences a sudden increase in market share than they would be in a more stable period. It is especially in such unstable periods that investors will be more likely to be influenced by the speculation of other investors, leading to herd effects and the type of over-reactions emphasized by Shiller (1989).

Although in periods of market share instability each firm individually has a stronger prospect for growth than in a more stable period, such growth prospects might be counteracted in the investor's mind by his/her inability to make predictions. The higher risk characteristic of the early phase of the industry life-cycle should cause the *P/E* ratio to be relatively lower in this period due to the reasons outlined above.

Kester (1984) offers an alternative view in his emphasis on the need for investors to balance considerations from net present value analysis and those from *expected future* growth analysis. While the former is better for simple growth options (from routine cost reduction, replacement projects and so on), the latter is better for 'compound growth options' (from research and development, entry into a new market and so on). Although his study focusses on the evaluation of investment projects, the analysis is useful for understanding the role of risk on stock prices. He states that it is often the smaller firms that have the highest growth opportunities (almost entirely based on future growth potential rather than on current cash flow). As an example, he cites an executive of a major consumer products company:

> If you know everything there is to know about a [new] product, it's not going to be a good business. There have to be some major uncertainties to be resolved. This is the only way to get a product with a major profit opportunity. (Kester, 1984, p. 157)

Hence in this alternative view, strong instability of market shares and earnings might represent the type of uncertainty signaling growth *opportunities*, causing the firm's price–earnings ratio to be higher. Interestingly, Kester ends his article (p. 160) with a very similar question to that posed in the present study: 'What influence do industry structure and competitive interaction have on growth option value?'. He states that the answer will vary from one situation and industry to another.

Lastly, in terms of the variance of stock prices *across* firms, the above analysis might also prove useful. If periods of market share instability (signaling future growth opportunities for firms which are currently not leaders) cause investors to have less confidence to bet too strongly for the firms who currently have attractive cash flows, the dispersion of stock prices and price–earnings between firms should be lower in the unstable period than in the more stable period.

4.3 Hypotheses: Co-evolution of Market Share Instability and Stock Price Volatility

Having reviewed the evolution of market share instability over the industry life-cycle and the possible effect of market share instability on stock prices, we now state some possible hypotheses that emerge from that discussion. The hypotheses are stated informally due to the fact that there is no commonly accepted theory of stock price determination, and also because market share and stock price volatility have not been connected in either the industrial organization or finance literature. The main contribution of the life-cycle literature is to provide insight into the industry-specific factors which affect the evolution of market share instability over time and/or among industries. If there is a relationship between market share instability and stock price volatility, then there are reasons to believe that the degree of excess volatility may also be affected by industry-specific factors. The hypotheses stimulate the questions asked in the empirical analysis in Section 5, which address each of these hypotheses.

1. *Evolution of firm numbers, output and stock prices over the life-cycle*
   Based on case studies, life-cycle theory predicts that at the beginning of most industries' history there is a rapid entry of firms, then a mass exit

(shakeout) and finally a stabilization in the number of firms. As stated above, Jovanovic and MacDonald (1994b) relate the shakeout to changes in the stock price index. Just before the shakeout the index falls due to the bad news of the innovation for incumbents. Then as some firms establish themselves as winners of the innovation race, the index rises (reflecting those firms' increase in value). Finally the index falls as the innovation diffuses and dissipates the rents by early innovators. Although the above dynamic can mean that market share instability affects changes in stock prices (for example, stock price volatility), the level of price–earnings, and inter-firm variance of stock prices and price–earnings, there is no clear reason why it should affect the stock price *level*.

2. *Market share instability and stock price volatility*   Market share instability is higher in the first phase of an industry's life-cycle due to the effect of entry, changing demand and changing technology. The uncertainty which results from such market share instability might cause stock prices to fluctuate more than in stable periods due to the uncertain profit opportunities.

3. *Excess volatility*   In the phase characterized by market share instability, the degree to which stock prices are more volatile than fundamentals should be higher than in more stable periods due to the greater difficulty in predicting firms' growth potentials. In this phase, since current performance is not a good predictor of future performance, even if a firm has strong earnings or dividends, its stock price may be abnormally high or low depending on the particular expectations regarding that firm's future growth. Expectation formation is likely to be dependent on the type of social interactions and 'over-reactions', described by Shiller (1989), *more* in unstable periods than in more stable periods. In the more stable periods, investors can more confidently use current performance indicators as predictors of future performance.

4. *Level of price-earnings*   The level of price–earnings is related to the concept of excess volatility since it captures the difference between expected performance (stock price, P) and real performance (earnings, E). But whereas excess volatility refers to the changes in stock prices, which indeed should be more volatile during unstable periods due to the over-reactions and constant corrections referred to above, the level of price–earnings captures the absolute difference between actual and speculated performance and is hence less clearly affected by unstable periods. Its level during unstable periods will depend on the particular interpretation of uncertainty by investors; on the one hand, greater variance in firm growth prospects causes the horizon for which growth can be forecasted to fall and hence the price–earnings to fall (Malkiel and Cragg, 1970). On the other hand, the fact that uncertainty is often associated with greater profit opportunity for individual firms might cause the price–earnings to rise (Kester, 1984).

5. *Variance* The variance *across* firm stock prices might be higher in the more stable (mature) phase of the industry life-cycle because it is easier for investors to make predictions on future winners and losers (Klein, 1977). This gives them more confidence to give a higher than average stock price to a firm with a currently high market share, as opposed to an unstable phase where it is not so clear that high market share today means high market share tomorrow. This should cause the inter-firm variance to be lower in the unstable period due to the more cautious speculation.

5 EMPIRICAL ANALYSIS: THE US AUTOMOBILE INDUSTRY

We now turn to the data. We look at firm market shares, stock prices and earnings in the US automobile industry from 1921 to 1995. We ask to what degree the volatility in market shares is correlated with the volatility of stock prices and with the price–earnings level. The data are divided into firm- and industry-level data.

5.1 Description of the Data

Firm level data The firm level market share data were taken from *Ward's Automotive Yearbook* and were adjusted to include only the fraction of each firm's production in total US production.[7] For each firm, the average yearly stock price was taken from the *New York Times* quotation which occurred usually around 3 or 4 January of the following year. The earnings/share data were taken from annual editions of *Moody's Industrial Manual* (1921–97). Each variable was adjusted for stock splits. The firm level price–earnings ratios were calculated by dividing each firm's stock price by the firm's earnings per share (each adjusted by their S&P counterpart). The statistical results from the firm-level data are reported in Table 4.1, below.

Which firms were included We collected data for the majority of US automobile firms which were quoted in the stock market. The full list, obtained from *Standard & Poor's Analyst Handbook*, includes (dates in parentheses refer to the date that the firm started being quoted): Chrysler (18 Dec. 1925), Ford Motor (29 Aug. 1956), General Motors (2 Jan. 1918), American Motors (5 May 1954 to 5 Aug. 1987), Auburn Automobile (31 Dec. 1925 to 4 May 1938), Chandler-Cleveland (2 Jan. 1918 to 28 Dec. 1925), Hudson Motor Car (31 Dec. 1925 to 28 April 1954), Hupp Motor Car (2 Jan. 1918 to 17 Jan. 1940), Nash-Kelvinator Corp (31 Dec. 1925 to 28 April 1954), Packard Motor Car (7 Jan. 1920 to 29 Sept. 1954), Pierce-Arrow (2 Jan. 1918 to 28 Dec. 1925),

Reo Motor Car (31 Dec. 1925 to 17 Jan. 1940), Studebaker Corp. (6 Oct. 1954 to 22 April 1964),[8] White Motor (2 Jan. 1918 to 2 Nov. 1932), and Willy's Overland (2 Jan. 1918 to 29 March 1933). Of these, we did *not* include in our analysis Auburn, Chandler, Pierce, Reo and White, either because of the unavailability of data for these firms or due to the extremely short time period during which their shares were traded. Although Ford began to be publicly traded only in 1956, we included it in the sample because of its importance in the US auto industry. We did not adjust for mergers. The only adjustment made was for stock splits. For example, after General Motors merged with American Motors (in 1987), the stock price data for General Motors includes that of American Motors, but an adjustment was made for the 2:1 stock split which followed the merger.

Industry-level data   Average stock price data from 1921 to 1995 are from *Standard and Poor's Analyst Handbook*. The firms included by *Standard & Poor's* to calculate the industry average are those listed in the paragraph above. Since the corresponding average dividend/share and earnings/share data are not available from *Standard & Poor's* for the whole time period (only from 1946 onwards), we derive the average dividend/share and earnings/share data from 1921 to 1995 by averaging across firms using the firm-level data we collected.

Detrending   Stock prices, price–earnings ratios and dividends for US automobile firms, as well as for the industry as a whole (aggregate data), are divided by their S&P 500 composite counterpart to isolate the dynamics of the automobile industry from the dynamics of the economy as a whole. Furthermore, when computing correlations and standard deviations, the variables (including market shares) are de-trended by an *exponential* trend line. This ensures that the series are stationary and hence comparable (as in Shiller, 1989).[9] The results from the industry-level analysis are found in Tables 4.2 and 4.3, below.

Sub-periods   To capture the life-cycle concept we analyse the co-evolution of financial and industrial dynamics in two distinct periods. The total time span comprising both periods was chosen to coincide with the years in which *both* financial (stock prices, dividends) and industrial (market share, earnings) data were available. So although the Ford Motor Company was established in 1903, since it only went public in 1956, we start the analysis of Ford in 1956 when both sets of data are available. Having chosen the total time period, we then divide this period into two to look at the first half of the firm's history compared to its second half. Data for the entire period are also included. This procedure makes the dating of the two phases differ across firms depending on the firm's founding date, the date at which the firm went public, and the date when the firm ceased to exist (either due to a merger or to an exit).

The same division is performed for the industry-level data (early stage of the life-cycle, mature phase of the life-cycle). The resulting three periods are 1921–58, 1959–95 and 1921–95. The two phases at the firm level will thus not necessarily coincide with the dating of the phases for the industry life-cycle. Yet the phases are divided in this way to avoid an arbitrary choice of years to include and also to include as many years as possible for each firm. These qualifications suggest that perhaps the *two most interesting firms to look at when interpreting the firm-level data are General Motors and Chrysler* precisely because their early founding date and the early date at which their shares went public make the division of their particular life-cycle coincide with that of the aggregate industry life-cycle. For these same reasons, we shall *de-emphasize the results that pertain to Kaiser (due to the few years for which data is available) and to Ford (due to the very late date at which it went public)*. It was in fact tempting to report only the results for General Motors and Chrysler but given the fact that data were collected for other firms as well, we thought that illustrating the patterns for other firms could only add to the insight gained from the exercise.

5.2 Analysis of Results

Below we report the results from the data analysis and compare them to the hypotheses listed in Section 4.3 (with the same numbering).

1. *Evolution of firm numbers, industry output and stock price*   Figure 4.2, above, documents the evolution of the number of automobile producers from 1904 to 1995: a steady rise until 1909 and then a steady fall (except for a short period in the late 1920s) until the present day. Figure 4.3 shows that (a) during this time, the average industry stock price first rose (from 1921 to the early 1970s) and then fell (from the late 1970s to the present); and (b) the total number (actual units) of automobiles sold/year rose steadily but at a decreasing rate.

   The relationship between the industry shakeout and the fall in the stock price predicted by Jovanovic and MacDonald (1994b) is hard to detect in the data since the shakeout in this industry occurred between 1909 and 1926 and our average stock price index data only begin in 1918 (in 1918 the number of producers was already half of what it was in 1909). Figure 4.3 indicates that a long-term fall in stock price started around 1960, but Jovanovic and MacDonald (1994b) do not address changes over such a long period. The large bump in stock price between 1926 and 1932, however, does coincide with the change in technology from the Model T to the new 'heavier, closed body more comfortable car' and the associated

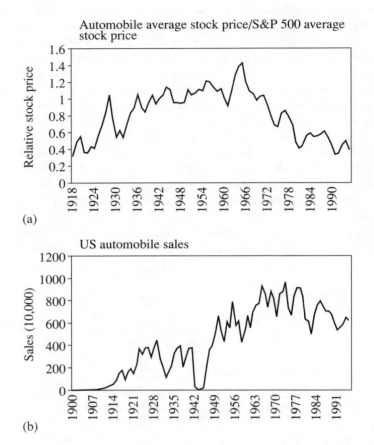

Source: Data on vehicle sales from *Ward's Automotive Yearbook* (1996, p. 19).

Figure 4.3   *Automobile average stock price/S&P 500 average stock price and US automobile sales*

change in market leadership referred to in Section 3 (Abernathy and Wayne, 1974). Future research can perhaps look at this particular period more closely to draw an association with the innovation dynamics described in Jovanovic and MacDonald (1994b). Nevertheless, as stated in Section 4, there is no a priori reason to believe that market share instability should affect the average *level* of stock price. There are, however, reasons to believe that it can affect excess volatility, the level of price–earnings and inter-firm variance of firm stock prices and price–earnings. We look at these below.

2. *Market share instability and stock price volatility*

Firm-level data Columns 2, 3, 5, 6 and 8 in Table 4.1 report the volatility of (de-trended) variables by analysing the standard deviation of their values over time. The value of 0.5602 for GM in column 3 means that between 1921 and 1958 the standard deviation of GM's annual price–earnings ratio was 0.5602. In columns 2, 3 and 5 we see that the standard deviation of market shares, price–earnings, and stock prices for most firms are higher in the first half of their history. The notable exception is Studebaker, which has a much higher standard deviation of price–earnings in the second phase. The other exceptions either have a minimal difference between the two phases, or else pertain to the two firms which we are de-emphasizing (Ford and Kaiser). Hence the overall level of volatility seems to be higher in the early phase of each firm's life-cycle.

Industry-level data Column 1 in Table 4.2 indicates that market share instability (calculated via equation (2.1)) is higher in the first phase (14.082) compared to the second phase (6.344), a result also shown graphically in Figure 4.1, above. The instability index for stock prices and price–earnings is also calculated using equation (2.1) except that instead of market shares it is the *relative* values of stock prices and price–earnings that are used (for example, each firm's stock price divided by the *industry* average stock price). The use of relative stock prices and price–earnings captures the changes *between* firms independent of the change experienced on average by all firms, and allows direct comparison with the instability index of market shares which are *relative* by nature.

In columns 4 and 5 of Table 4.2 we see that the average price–earnings ratio has a higher standard deviation in the first phase (1.4198 versus 0.9658) while the average stock price has a higher standard deviation in the second phase (0.1996 versus 0.1594). While column 5 indicates that the second period is characterized by greater variation of stock prices experienced by *all* firms, column 6 indicates that there is more variation *among* firms in the first period. The fact that the instability index of stock prices is much higher in the first phase is, as postulated in Section 4.3, probably connected to the greater degree of market share instability in that phase. In the case of price–earnings, the exact opposite holds: while the first phase is characterized by a higher standard deviation of average price–earnings, the second stage is characterized by a higher instability index of price–earnings. This suggests that the period characterized by relative stability in market shares causes price–earnings differences between firms to be more unstable. One reason for this might be that investors react more strongly to changes in firm earnings in the period in which market shares are relatively stable due to the greater confidence they have in those performance measures as indicators of future performance. This would cause changes in earnings to

Table 4.1 Firm-level data

1	2	3	4	5	6	7	8
	Stdev. ms	Stdev. p/e	Avg. p/e	Stdev. P	Stdev EMM	Exc. volat.	Stdev. ms–stdev. sp
GM							
1921–58	0.2263	0.5602	0.6508	0.7563	0.3159	0.4403	–0.53
1959–95	0.1067	0.6784	1.324	0.5062	0.5687	–0.0625	–0.3995
1921–95	0.1768	0.6277	0.9829	0.6445	0.4734	0.1711	–0.4677
Ford							
1956–76	0.1147	0.7667	1.128	0.2128	0.2083	0.0044	–0.0981
1977–95	0.133	0.7427	0.9442	0.492	0.3474	0.1146	–0.359
1956–95	0.1243	0.7481	1.043	0.373	0.2846	0.0884	–0.2487
Chrysler							
1925–56	0.4417	0.7185	2.18	0.7756	0.3697	0.4058	–0.3339
1957–95	0.1132	0.4151	0.3355	0.3963	0.2097	0.1866	–0.2831
1925–95	0.3366	0.6346	1.271	0.6729	0.3136	0.3592	–0.3363
American							
1955–70	0.4314	2	0.6188	0.3888	0.1589	0.2299	0.0426
1971–86	0.3259	1.058	0.9758	0.2616	0.3235	–0.0619	0.0643
1955–86	0.3767	1.594	0.809	0.3278	0.2562	0.0716	0.0489
Nash							
1927–37	1.29	0.9235	0.9113	1.864	0.348	1.5166	–0.574
1938–52	0.3256	0.4696	0.453	0.1462	0.2914	–0.1452	0.1794
1927–52	0.9237	0.7446	0.6821	1.4501	0.3073	1.1428	–0.5264
Hudson							
1925–37	0.3382	1.095	0.7686	0.6565	0.7202	–0.0636	–0.3183
1938–53	0.3278	0.4412	0.4125	0.5632	2.678	–2.114	–0.2354
1925–53	0.3313	0.887	0.6054	0.6057	3.131	–2.52	–0.2744
Packard							
1922–35	0.3216	1.4227	1.303	1.1	0.1749	0.9258	–0.7784
1936–53	0.4941	0.6046	1.308	0.3806	0.2562	0.1244	0.1135
1922–53	0.4311	1.0759	1.306	0.8092	0.2164	0.5927	–0.3781
Studebaker							
1922–40	0.2254	1.3124	0.668	0.8552	0.209	0.6461	–0.6298
1941–64	0.1621	3.9301	0.9884	0.7971	0.2236	0.5735	–0.635
1922–64	0.2393	2.9614	0.8371	0.8151	0.2198	0.5953	–0.5758
Willy's							
1936–46	0.5753	1.422	0.4196	1.2798		–7045	
1947–52	0.3686	0.9624	0.2281	1.5314			–1.1628
1936–52	0.4732	1.1926	0.3239	1.3893			–0.9161
Kaiser							
1948–51	0.6095	0.4006	0.0718	0.2353			0.3742
1952–54	1.239	2.0699	0.05	0.2059			1.0331
1948–54	0.846	1.3216	0.0625	0.215			0.631

Notes:

Column 1 Three phases: 1st and 2nd half, and total number of years during which firm was quoted.

Column 2 Standard deviation of de-trended market shares.

Column 3 Standard deviation of de-trended price–earnings.

Column 4 Average level of price–earnings.

Column 5 Standard deviation of de-trended stock price.

Column 6 Standard deviation of de-trended market value derived from EMM.

Column 7 Difference between 5 and 6 = excess volatility.

Column 8 Difference between standard deviation of market shares (2) and standard deviation of stock prices (5).

Table 4.2   Industry-level data

	1 MS ins.	2 Avg. P/E	3 Avg. SP	4 Stdev. P/E	5 Stdev. SP	6 SP ins.	7 P/E ins.
1921–58	14.082	1.879	0.9805	1.4198	0.1594	6.1659	1.1567
1959–95	6.3447	0.83	0.8719	0.9658	0.1996	0.2334	1.424
1921–95	10.324	1.3622	0.9277	1.3192	0.1869	3.2844	1.2865

Notes:
Column 1   Market share instability index.
Column 2   Average price–earnings.
Column 3   Average stock price.
Column 4   Standard deviation of de-trended price–earnings.
Column 5   Standard deviation of de-trended stock price.
Column 6   Stock price instability index (relative).
Column 7   Price–earnings instability index (relative).

be accompanied, perhaps with a lag, by changes in stock prices *more* in the stable period than in the unstable period. The fact that such changes in prices and earnings will not necessarily be proportional to each other, nor constant over time, will only add to the instability of price–earnings. Hence even if the instability index of stock prices is higher in the more unstable period, the particular way in which stock prices react to changes in earnings could make the instability index of price–earnings higher in the period in which market shares are more stable.

3. *Excess volatility*   To measure excess volatility we compare the standard deviation of actual stock prices to the standard deviation of the EMM price. As in Shiller (1989), it is the *de-trended* values of both stock prices and the EMM price that we analyse. The EMM price is calculated using equation (4.4) in Section 2. We use earnings/share instead of dividends/share because of their greater availability, but as already mentioned in Section 2, Shiller's studies have found that this does not make a difference on the degree of excess volatility (Shiller, 1989). Although we use a discount rate of 0.05, the qualitative results are insensitive to the particular rate used.

We first look at the *existence* of excess volatility in the US automobile industry and then look at the *degree* of excess volatility in different sub-periods. At the firm level, the presence of excess volatility is seen in Table 4.1, column 7 where the difference between the standard deviation of the actual price and the standard deviation of the EMM price is calculated. For each firm, except Hudson, the difference for the overall period is positive, meaning that on average stock prices are more volatile than the EMM price, that is, excess volatility exists.

As regards the different sub-periods, column 7 indicates that the difference between the standard deviation of the actual price and the standard deviation of the EMM price is higher for all firms, except Ford and Hudson, in the first phase. In the case of Ford the exception is not terribly informative since its first phase occurs relatively late in its history. Hence in general, excess volatility is larger in the first phase of each firm's history. We provided a possible reason for this in point 3 of Section 4.3.

Another aspect of excess volatility can be captured by comparing the variance in market shares to the variance in stock prices. Column 8 calculates the difference between the standard deviation of (de-trended) market shares and the standard deviation of (de-trended) stock prices. For almost every firm (except American and Kaiser), the standard deviation of market shares is much smaller than the standard deviation of stock prices (indicated by the negative sign). The degree to which stock prices are more volatile than market shares is higher in the first phase of the life-cycle for most (relevant) firms. Using an evolutionary simulation model, Mazzucato and Semmler (1997) show that this result is exactly the opposite of the result which emerges from the Efficient Market Model.[10] All these results indicate that in the period in which market shares are more unstable, stock prices are more volatile than real performance measures (earnings, dividends and market shares).

4. *Average price–earnings*   In Table 4.1, column 4, the average level of the price–earnings ratio is higher for some firms in the first half of their history (Ford, Chrysler, Nash, Hudson, Willys), and larger for other firms in the second half (GM, American, Studebaker). In column 2 of Table 4.2 we see that the average price–earnings for the whole industry was quite a bit higher in the first phase (1.879) than in the second phase (0.83). A higher price–earnings in a period characterized by market instability (uncertainty) runs counter to arguments in finance theory that predict the price–earnings ratio to be lower during more uncertain periods due to the reduced ability of investors to predict growth prospects of firms (Malkiel and Cragg, 1970). On the other hand, this result accords with Kester's (1984) view that price–earnings ratios should be highest in periods of uncertainty due to the greater growth prospects which such periods offer.

5. *Variance in firm stock prices*   Columns 1–3 in Table 4.3 show still another type of volatility: the variance *across* firms in market shares, stock prices and price–earnings.[11] The focus here is on the differences across firms at one point in time and the evolution of those differences over time. Variances are computed annually and then averaged over each of the three periods. Columns 1–3 in the table indicate that the average dispersion of market shares, stock prices and price–earnings was lower in 1921–58 than in 1959–95.

Table 4.3   Variance between firms (with standard deviations in parentheses)

	1 Avg. var. MS	2 Avg. var. P/E	3 Avg. var. SP
1921–58	0.294 (0.16)	0.0351 (0.1803)	0.0237 (0.1440)
1959–95	0.463 (0.21)	0.0579 (0.2196)	0.0313 (0.1666)
1921–95	0.378 (0.19)	0.047 (0.2008)	0.0274 (0.1550)

Notes:
Column 1   Average of inter-firm market share variance.
Column 2   Average of inter-firm (relative) P/E variance.
Column 3   Average of inter-firm (relative) stock price variance.

This result was predicted in hypothesis 5, section 4.3, where it was argued that in the later period in the industry life-cycle, when market shares are more stable and market concentration is higher (supported by different life-cycle theories), investors have more reason to use current market share as an indicator of future performance and hence to give a consistently higher market value to firms which are current leaders. This causes the dispersion of market values to increase in the later stage of an industry's evolution. We show the result graphically in Figure 4.4, where we see a rising trend (the dotted line represents a linear trend).

6   CONCLUSION

Empirical studies have linked market share instability to industry-specific factors, such as the period in the industry life-cycle and the type of 'technological regime'. Market share instability tends to be higher in the beginning stage of the industry life-cycle, and in industries characterized by high entry, the lack of persistence in innovation and a codifiable knowledge base (Klepper, 1996; Malerba and Orsenigo, 1996). The 'excess volatility' of stock prices has been connected to the general 'over-reaction' of investors (Shiller, 1989). We focussed on the relationship between market share instability and stock price volatility to study whether industry specific factors might also affect 'excess volatility'.

The empirical analysis of the US automobile industry suggests that there are distinct patterns in the evolution of stock price volatility over the life-cycle, and hence that the *degree* of excess volatility might be influenced by industry-specific phenomena. The finding that excess volatility is higher in the first phase of each firm's history suggests that market share instability produces a form of 'uncertainty' which makes predictions about future growth rates more

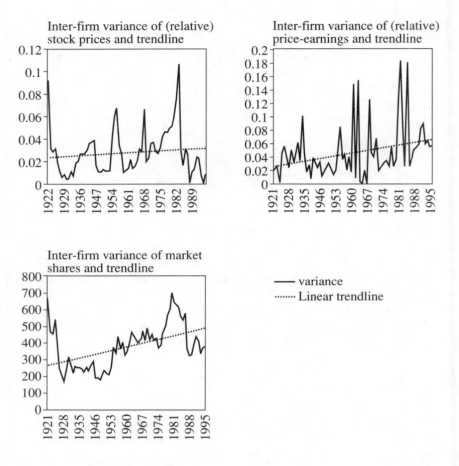

*Figure 4.4   Inter-firm variance of stock prices, price–earnings and market
shares*

difficult and hence market values more turbulent than real performance
measures (dividends or earnings). The finding that average price–earnings are
higher in the first phase suggests that the greater uncertainty of this period
might have caused investors to foresee more general growth opportunities
(Kester, 1984). The greater variance *across* firms in their market shares, stock
prices and price–earnings in the later phase of the life-cycle suggests that in the
phase in which market shares are more stable, investors are more willing to
make strong bets for/against specific firms due to their greater confidence in
being able to predict the future performance of these firms.

Although the results are rough and pertain to only one industry, we hope that they will stimulate new stylized facts regarding the financial side of the life-cycle to be added to the ones we already know concerning the 'real' side (Gort and Klepper, 1982; Klepper, 1996). The Schumpeterian literature that identifies and categorizes the differences in technological patterns and 'regimes' in particular industries over time, as well as across industries during specific periods in time, can provide a useful framework for such future research.

NOTES

* This chapter was co-written with W. Semmler, and reprinted here from the *Journal of Evolutionary Economics*, 1999, Vol. 9 (1): 67–96, with permission from Springer-Verlag.

1. Even in the years around the Great Depression, dividends and earnings did not increase wildly when the stock market peaked around 1929, nor did they fall abruptly when the stock market fell dramatically in 1932 (Shiller, 1989).

2. Shiller's studies (1989) have shown the result of excess volatility to be insensitive to the particular discount rate chosen. He also experiments with time-varying discount rates, where the variation is approximated by changes in real consumption data. He finds that such variation does not alter the results on excess volatility (Shiller, 1989, p. 115). The only way that the stock prices generated from the EMM can be made to be as volatile as real stock prices is to make the discount rate vary greatly at each point in time, a highly unrealistic assumption. To conclude, he states: 'The movements in expected real interest rates that would justify the variability in stock prices are very large – much larger than the movements in nominal interest rates over the sample period' (pp. 124–5).

3. They admit that this is a strong assumption but one that is supported by the fact that a single shakeout is typical in the Gort and Klepper (1982) data and that particularly in the US tire industry there seems to have been one major invention, the Banbury mixer in 1916, which caused the shakeout to occur (Jovanovic and MacDonald, 1994b, pp. 324–5). Klepper and Simons (1997) argue against this assumption.

4. The firm earnings/share figures used in Section (5) to calculate price–earnings are those reported in *Moody's Manual of Investment*. These are earnings *net of interest paid to bondholders*. This is important since earnings/share will otherwise be affected by the finance structure of firms (for example, their debt/equity ratio).

5. Malkiel and Cragg (1970) explain: 'the horizon, N, over which firm growth prospects can be forecasted is itself a function of the variance of the returns stream. Hence investors would project extraordinary earnings growth over only a very limited horizon for companies where the anticipated variance of the earnings stream is large. Since it can be shown that $\delta(P/E)/\delta N > 0$, it follows that price–earnings should be negatively related to the variance term' (1970, p. 602).

6. They stress, for example, Keynes's idea of the 'beauty contest' where the rational contestant would not pick those girls that he himself found prettiest, but those that he anticipated the other contestants would believe the *average* opinion would consider prettiest: 'We conclude that if one wants to explain returns over a one-year horizon it is far more important to know what the market will think the growth rate of earnings will be next year rather than to know the realized long term growth rate' (Malkiel and Cragg, 1970, p. 616).

7. We provided a justification for this in Section 2, above.

8. Formerly Studebaker-Packard.

9. Different de-trending procedures, such as dividing by a linear, moving average or a log-normal trendline, could have been used. Campbell and Shiller (1988) de-trend stock prices by dividing them by a long moving average of lagged dividends. Since these long moving averages are fairly smooth and trendlike, dividing price by such a moving average is a method

of detrending or of removing low-frequency components. Mankiw et al. (1985) instead de-trend by using a proportional-to-dividend rule for price. We did not consider using any type of *constant* trend, such as the last mentioned or the linear trend, since real dividend series are not smooth at all (linear trend lines bias the results if there is non-stationarity in levels). We found that de-trending with a moving average trendline or an exponential trendline did not produce different qualitative results.

10. Mazzucato and Semmler (1997) build a simulation model which (a) reproduces empirical regularities in market share patterns by exploring different Schumpeterian scenarios connecting the evolution of market shares to firms' rates of cost reduction (innovation), and (b) embodies assumptions from the EMM to make predictions regarding the difference between market share instability and stock price volatility. The EMM is used as a benchmark case as in Shiller (1989). In relating market shares to innovation, the model embodies arguments found in Abernathy and Wayne (1974) and Klein (1977) by assuming that in the first stage of the life-cycle there is negative feedback (as market share rises the rate of cost reduction falls) while in the later stage there is positive feedback. While the model generates market share patterns resembling the actual ones observed, the EMM fails to generate the empirical patterns of market values; the model predicts market shares and profits (a proxy for dividends) to be more volatile than market values and the difference to be higher in the first phase of the industry. The empirical results reviewed above indicate the opposite to be true. For a copy of the paper please contact the authors directly.

11. The same general patterns were found using the standard deviation instead of the variance.

Concluding statement

The following statement provides some general thoughts on the issues raised and results obtained from the previous four chapters. More specific conclusions can be found at the end of each chapter.

We began by presenting empirical facts on the dynamics of firm size, market structure and innovation. These included two main qualitative features: (1) the non-linear nature of the relationship between the three variables, and (2) the fact that relatively stable regularities (such as the skewed size distribution of firms) emerge from a relatively unstable and heterogeneous micro structure. The nature of these phenomena provided strong motivation for developing an evolutionary perspective on industrial change along with dynamic techniques appropriate for exploring and modeling such change. When systems are characterized by non-linearities and complexity (where by the latter we mean the interwoven relationship between micro interactions and emergent macro patterns), conventional tools based on optimization, linearity and predictability are not appropriate for exploring evolution. Not only are closed-form analytical solutions often not calculable for such systems, but even when they are they are unable to give us much information about *evolution* over time (only about some points around an equilibrium).

Computer simulation methods were used due to their ability to: (a) solve a large system of non-linear differential equations, (b) allow step-by-step inclusion of different levels of complexity (stochastic shocks, more agents, industry-specific variables), and (c) trace the evolution of market structures, with emphasis on the *patterns* not just the final state, which emerge from the non-linear relationship between firm size and innovation. The combination of these factors allowed a typology of market structures to be constructed, matching different parameter values to market characteristics.

To emphasize the necessity for an alternative theoretical and modeling approach, we began by outlining the difference between static and dynamic approaches to the study of firm size and market structure. It was found that the former, by the very fact that the focus is on *given* techniques of production, cannot address the role of innovation dynamics in producing the stylized facts of market concentration and instability. One of the more dynamic views of market structure was found in industry life-cycle theories which study how the relationship between firm size and innovation evolves over time. The models developed in Chapters 2 and 3 incorporated the hypothesis that in the early stage of industry evolution it is small flexible firms that are better innovators since the uncertain (changing) demand and technological standards in this stage require firms to *explore* new frontiers of production rather than to *exploit* existing ones. Alternatively, in the later more mature stage, when both demand and technology are more stable, it is larger firms that have the competitive advantage due to their greater ability to exploit economies of scale. The models explored the implications of these assumptions under different parameter settings, where the latter included: the average rate of cost reduction in the industry, the initial variety of efficiency levels, and the size of shocks to costs.

The simulation analysis separated static from dynamic analysis and stochastic from deterministic analysis. The former distinction allowed us to explore the relationship between firm size, the *direction* of costs and the *rate* of cost reduction. The analysis of *dynamic* returns to scale found that negative feedback should not be dismissed as less interesting than positive feedback (as it usually is), since it provides insight into the possible causes of market share instability. The results are summarized in the Introduction of the book as well as at the end of Chapters 2 and 3.

The link between the deterministic and the stochastic analysis in Chapters 2 and 3 allows a better understanding of which aspects of market disequilibria emerge from the non-linear (deterministic) relation between firm size and innovation, and which aspects are instead caused by the idiosyncratic nature of change. This allows the elements of 'chance' and 'necessity' in industrial evolution to be studied systematically, with neither one taking center stage. The *degree* to which idiosyncratic events affect deterministic dynamics under different regimes of innovation was explored in Chapter 3. It was found that shocks have the greatest effect under the following conditions: during the regime of negative feedback; when the average speed of cost reduction in the industry is neither too low nor too high; and when the size of the shocks are neither too small nor too large.

Chapter 4 explored how the varying degrees of predictability in the industry life-cycle can affect the way that the stock market determines values for particular firms. Since a period of high market share instability is a period in which current market shares do not act as good predictors of future market shares, the results in Chapter 2 suggest that predictability should be lower when it is small firms that are better innovators (negative feedback). Although it is evident that there are many random factors that influence stock market volatility, the object of Chapter 4 was to see whether the degree to which stock prices are volatile (over time and across firms) varies over the industry life-cycle. If part of the randomness affecting stock prices has to do with how investors form expectations, and if the changing degree of predictability is tied to the evolving relationship between innovation and firm size, then the changing degree of predictability over the industry life-cycle must certainly play a role in determining stock price volatility. The empirical study of the US automobile industry confirms this with results that suggest that industry-specific factors affect the *degree* of stock price volatility. The chapter bridges the quasi-deterministic theories of stock prices which link stock prices only to fundamentals (the net present value of dividend payments), with quasi-stochastic theories of stock prices which instead link stock prices to social factors like animal spirits and so on. *As in Chapter 3, we find here that economic evolution is determined neither by purely structural nor by purely idiosyncratic processes, but by the dynamic interaction between the two.*

The issue of predictability carries implications for industrial policy. If, as was found in Chapter 2, periods of negative feedback cause the current ranking of firms to be a bad indicator of future ranking, should a firm's current monopoly power be used against it? Under such conditions, are subsidies to small firms necessary since it is those same firms that might 'naturally' rise to the top? The identification of certain types of industries and/or periods in the industry life-cycle with particular types of positive or negative feedback as well as with other industry-specific factors (for example, slow or fast average rates of cost reduction), allows the present analysis to usefully inform such questions.

The research initiated here can be extended in various ways. The most obvious extension is the inclusion of more variables into the models. Chapters 2 and 3 focussed on building reduced-form models so that general results could be attained. This was deemed necessary since adding too many firm-specific and stochastic variables from the start hides whether the results which emerge are due to the characteristics of the underlying non-linear model or to the introduction of idiosyncratic elements. Having now cleared the ground by specifying the deterministic results and the degree to which stochastic shocks affect those results, new variables can be introduced. Price dynamics can be introduced in a way that makes prices a function of both random and structural elements: for example, firms on the one hand face the pressure (necessity) to charge a price which will not 'select' them out of the market, while, on the other hand, the current market structure determines the degree of freedom (chance) that firms have in choosing a price which differs from that competitive price. Other possible additions include entry and exit dynamics, and shocks that instead of being exogenous have moments which are functions of the current market structure and firm ranking. For example, the probability that a new firm enters and/or the probability that large or small firms are better innovators could be made a function of the current (and changing) degree of concentration and instability.

Appendix

PROOF OF EQUATIONS (2.1a) AND (2.4)

Equation (2.1a) follows directly from equation (2.1). For the case of n firms, we have:

$$\sum_{i=1}^{n} s_i = 1 \qquad \text{(A.1)}$$

and

$$\dot{s}_i = \lambda s_i (\bar{c} - c_i) \quad i = 1,...,n. \qquad \text{(A.2)}$$

Sum (A.2) over i:

$$\sum \dot{s}_i = \lambda \sum s_i (\bar{c} - c_i). \qquad \text{(A.3)}$$

From (A.1) we have:

$$\sum_i \dot{s}_i = 0. \qquad \text{(A.4)}$$

Substitute into (A.3)

$$\bar{c} \sum s_i = \sum s_i c_i.$$

Therefore, using equation (2.1),

$$\bar{c} = \sum s_i c_i.$$

Proof of Equation (2.4),

$$s_1(t) = \left[1 + \frac{1 - s_1(0)}{s_1(0)} e^{-\beta t}\right]^{-1}.$$

$$\dot{s}_1 = \beta s_1(1 - s_1), \quad \text{where } \beta = \lambda\overline{\left(c_2 - c_1\right)}$$

$$\frac{ds_1}{s_1(1 - s_1)} = \beta dt \Rightarrow \int \frac{ds_1}{s_1(1 - s_1)} = \beta(t) =$$

$$\ln\left[\frac{s_1(t)}{s_1(0)} \cdot \frac{1 - s_1(0)}{1 - s_1(t)}\right] = \beta(t) \Rightarrow \frac{s_1(t)}{s_1(0)} \cdot \frac{1 - s_1(0)}{1 - s_1(t)} = e^{\beta t} \Rightarrow \frac{s_1(t)}{1 - s_1(t)} = \frac{s_1(0)}{1 - s_1(0)} e^{\beta t} \Rightarrow$$

$$\frac{1 - s_1(t)}{s_1(t)} = \frac{1 - s_1(0)}{s_1(0)} e^{-\beta t} \Rightarrow \frac{1}{s_1(t)} - 1 = \left[\frac{1}{s_1(0)} - 1\right] e^{-\beta t}$$

$$\frac{1}{s_1(t)} = 1 + \frac{1 - s_1(0)}{s_1(0)} e^{-\beta t} \Rightarrow s_1(t) = \left[1 + \frac{1 - s_1(0)}{s_1(0)} e^{-\beta t}\right]^{-1}.$$

Bibliography

Abernathy, W.J. and J.M. Utterback (1975), 'A dynamic model of product and process innovation', *Omega*, **3** (6): 424–41.

Abernathy, W.J. and K. Wayne (1974), 'Limits to the learning curve', *Harvard Business Review*, **52**: 109–20.

Ackert, L.F. and B.F Smith (1993), 'Stock price volatility, ordinary dividends, and other cash flows to shareholders', *Journal of Finance*, **48** (4): 1147–60.

Acs, Z.J. and D.B. Audretsch (1987), 'Innovation, market structure and firm size,' *Review of Economics and Statistics*, **69** (4): 567–74.

Acs, Z.J. and D.B. Audretsch (1990), *Innovation and Small Firms*, Cambridge, MA: MIT Press.

Arrow, K.J. (1962), 'Economic welfare and the allocation of resources for invention', in *The Rate and Invention of Economic Activity*, Universities National Bureau Committee for Economic Research, Princeton, NJ: Princeton University Press: pp. 155–73.

Arthur, B. (1989),'Competing technologies, increasing returns, and lock-in by historical small events', *Economic Journal*, **99**: 116–31.

Arthur, B. (1990), 'Positive feedbacks in the economy', *Scientific American*, February 92–9.

Arthur, B. (1994), *Increasing Returns and Path Dependence in the Economy*, Ann Arbor, MI: University of Michigan Press.

Arthur, B., I. Ermoliev and I. Kasniovski (1987), 'Path-dependent processes and the emergence of macro-structure', *European Journal of Operational Research*, **30** (3): 294–303.

Audretsch, D.B. (1995), *Innovation and Industry Evolution*, Cambridge, MA: MIT Press.

Bain, W. (1951), *Barriers to New Competition*, Cambridge, MA: Harvard University Press.

Baumol, W., J. Panzar and R. Willig (1982), *Contestable Markets and the Theory of Industry Structure*, New York: Harcourt Brace Jovanovich.

Beaver, W. and D. Morse (1978), 'What determines price–earnings ratios', *Financial Analysts Journal*, July–August: 65–76.

Berle, A.B. and G. Means (1932), *The Modern Corporation and Private Property*, New York: Macmillan.

Blitz, R., B. Bolch, P. Laux, and J. Siegfried (1987), 'The effect of structure on the cost of borrowing', in R. Willis, *Issues After a Century of Federal Competition Policy*, Lexington, MA: Lexington Books: pp. 333–44.

Bozeman, B., A. Link and A. Zardhoohi (1986), 'An economic analysis of R&D joint ventures', *Managerial and Decision Economics*, **7**: 263–66.

Brozen, Y. (1971), 'Concentration and structural and market disequilibria', *Antitrust Bulletin*, **16**: 244–8.

Cable, J. (1997), 'Market share behavior and mobility: an analysis and time-series application', *Review of Economics and Statistics*, **79**: 136–41.

Cable, J. (1998), 'Market share dynamics and competition: a survey of the empirical literature', Aberystwyth Economic Research Papers, University of Wales.

Campbell, J. and R. Shiller (1988), 'The dividend–price ratio and expectations of future dividends and discount factors', *Review of Financial Studies*, **14**: 195–228.

Christensen, C. (1997), *The Innovator's Dilemma: When New Technologies Cause Great Firms to Fail*, Boston, MA: HBS Press.

Cochrane, J.H. (1991), 'Volatility tests and efficient markets', *Journal of Monetary Economics*, **27** (3): 463–85.

Cohen, W.M. and R.C. Levin (1989), 'Empirical studies of innovation and market structure', in R. Schmalansee and R. Willig (eds), *Handbook of Industrial Organization*, Vol. 2, Vienna: North-Holland: 1059–107.

Cohen, W.M., R.C. Levin and D.C. Mowery (1987), 'Firm size and R&D intensity: a re-examination', *Journal of Industrial Economics*, **35**: 543–63.

Cohen, W. and D. Levinthal (1989), 'Innovation and learning: the two faces of R&D, implications for the analysis of R&D investment', *Economic Journal*, **99**: 569–96.

Collins, N.R. and L.E. Preston (1961), 'The size structure of the largest industrial firms,' *American Economic Review*, **51**: 986–1011.

Comanor, W.S. (1967), 'Market structure, product differentiation, and industrial research', *Quarterly Journal of Economics*, **85**: 524–31.

Dasgupta, P. and J. Stiglitz (1980), 'Industrial structure and the nature of innovative activity,' *Economic Journal*, **90**: 266–93.

Datta, Y. (1971), 'Competitive strategies and performance of firms in the US television set industry, 1950–60', PhD Dissertation, Business Administration Department, State University New York, Buffalo.

David, P. (1985), 'Clio and the economics of QWERTY', *American Economic Review*, **75**: 332–7.

David, P. (1994), 'Path dependency and predictability in dynamic systems with local network externalities: a paradigm for historical economics', in D. Foray and C. Freeman (eds), *Technology and the Wealth of Nations*, London: Pinter.

Demsetz, H. (1973), 'Industry structure, market rivalry, and public policy', *Journal of Law and Economics*, **16**: 1–9.

Dosi, G. (1984), *Technical Change and Industrial Transformation*, London: Macmillan.

Dosi, G. and C. Freeman (1988), *Technical Change and Economic Theory*, London: Pinter.

Dosi, G. and Y. Kaniovski (1994), 'The method of generalised urn schemes in the analysis of technological and economic dynamics', in G. Silverberg and L. Soete (eds), *The Economics of Growth and Technical Change: Technologies, Nations, Agents*, Aldershot, UK: Edward Elgar: pp. 261–84.

Dosi, G., Y.M. Kaniovski and S. Winter (1997b), 'A baseline model of industry evolution', IIASA Interim Report IR-97–013.

Dosi, G., F. Malerba, O. Marsili and L. Orsenigo (1997a), 'Industrial structures and dynamics: evidence, interpretations and puzzles', *Industrial and Corporate Change*, **6**: 1–22.

Dosi, G., O. Marsili, L. Orsenigo and R. Salvatore (1995), 'Learning, market selection and the evolution of industrial structures', *Small Business Economics*, **7**: 411–36.

Dosi, G. and L. Orsenigo (1987), 'Order and change: an exploration of markets, institutions and technology in industrial dynamics', Working Paper No. 110, Working Paper Series, Department of Economics, Washington University, St Louis, May.

Dosi, G. and L. Orsenigo (1988), 'Coordination and transformation: an overview of structures, behaviour and change in evolutionary environments', in G. Dosi and C. Freeman (eds), *Technical Change and Economic Theory*, London: Pinter.

Dosi, G., K. Pavitt and L. Soete (1988), *The Economics of Technical Change and International Trade*, Brighton, UK: Wheatsheaf.

England, R.W. (1994), *Evolutionary Concepts in Contemporary Economics*, Ann Arbor, MI: University of Michigan Press.

Epstein, R. (1928), *The Automobile Industry; Its Economic and Commercial Development*, New York: Arno Press.

Evans, D. (1987), 'The relationship between firm growth, size and age: estimates for 100 manufacturing industries', *Journal of Industrial Economics*, **35**: 567–81.

Federal Trade Commission, *Report on the Motor Vehicle Industry*, 76th Congress, First Session (1940), Washington, DC: House Document 468.

Fellner, W. (1951), 'The influence of market structure on technological progress', *Quarterly Journal of Economics*, **65**: 650–67.

Fisher, R.A. (1930), *The Genetic Theory of Natural Selection*, Oxford: Oxford University Press.

Foley, D. (1997), 'Long-range forecasting of economic policy impacts on the global environment', Barnard College Working Paper.

French, M.J. (1991), *The US Tire Industry*, Boston, MA: Twayne.

Galbraith, J.K. (1952), *American Capitalism*, Boston, MA: Houghton Mifflin.

Gellman Research Associates (1976), *Indicators of International Trends in Technological Innovation*, Final Report to the National Science Foundation, NTIS Document PB 263–738, Jenkintown, Pennsylvania.

Geroski, P. (1990), 'Innovation, technological opportunity and market structure', *Oxford Economic Papers*, **42**: 586–602.

Geroski, P. and S. Machin (1993), 'Innovation, profitability and growth over the business cycle', *Empirica*, **20**: 35–50.

Geroski, P., S. Machin and C. Walters (1997), 'Corporate growth and profitability', *Journal of Industrial Economics*, **65**: 171–89.

Geroski, P. and M. Mazzucato (1999), 'Myopic selection and the learning curve', London Business School, mimeo.

Geroski, P. and A. Pomroy (1990), 'Innovation and the evolution of market structure', *Journal of Industrial Economics*, **38**: 299–314.

Gibrat, R. (1931), *Les Inégalités Economiques*, Paris: Requeil Sirey.

Gleick, J. (1995), 'The Microsoft monopoly', *New York Times Magazine*, 5 November: 50–64.

Gort, M. (1963), 'Analysis of stability and change in market shares', *Journal of Political Economy*, **62**: 51–61.

Gort, M. and S. Klepper (1982), 'Time paths in the diffusion of product innovations', *Economic Journal*, **92**: 630–53.

Gort, M. and A. Konakayama (1982), 'A model of diffusion in the production of an innovation', *American Economic Review*, **72**: 1111–19.

Griliches, Z. (1979), 'Issues in assembling the contribution of research and development to productivity growth', *Bell Journal of Economics*, **10**: 92–116.

Grossack, I. (1965), 'Towards an integration of static and dynamic measures of industry concentration', *Review of Economics and Statistics*, **47**: 301–8.

Gruber, H. (1994), *Learning and Strategic Product Innovation; Theory and Evidence for the Semiconductor Industry*, Amsterdam: North-Holland.

Haken, H. (1978), *Synergetics: An Approach to Self Organization, in Self-Organizing Systems: The Emergence of Order*, Berlin: Plenum Press.

Haldi, J. and M. Whitcomb (1967), 'Economies of scale in industrial plants', *Journal of Political Economy*, **75**: 373–85.

Hall, B. (1987), 'The relationship between firm size and firm growth in the US manufacturing sector', *Journal of Industrial Economics*, **35**: 583–606.

Hamberg, D. (1964), 'Size of firm, oligopoly and research: the evidence', *Canadian Journal of Economics and Political Science*, **30**: 62–75.

Hamel, G. (1998), 'Opinion, strategy innovation and the quest for value', *Sloan Management Review*, Winter: 7–14.

Hannan, M. and J. Freeman (1984), 'Structural inertia and organizational change', *American Sociological Review*, **49**: 149–64.

Hannan, M.T. and J. Freeman (1989), *Organizational Ecology*, Cambridge, MA: Harvard University Press.

Hart, P.E. and S.J. Prais (1956), 'The analysis of business concentration', *Journal of the Royal Statistical Society*, **119** (2): 150–81.

Henderson, R. and K. Clark (1990), 'Architectural innovation: the reconfiguration of existing product technologies and the failure of established companies', *Administrative Science Quarterly*, **35**: 9–30.

Hergert, M. (1984), 'Market share and profitability: is bigger really better?', *Business Economics*, **5**: 45–8.

Hofbauer J. and K. Sigmund (1988), *Evolutionary Theory and Dynamic Systems*, Cambridge, MA: Cambridge University Press.

Horowitz, L. (1962), 'Firm size and research activity', *Southern Economic Journal*, **28**: 298–301.

Hymer S. and P. Pashigian (1962), 'Turnover of firms as a measure of market behavior', *Review of Economics and Statistics*, **44**: 82–7.

Ijiri, Y. and H. Simon (1977), *Skew Distributions and Sizes of Business Firms*, Amsterdam: North-Holland.

Iwai, K. (1984a), 'Schumpeterian dynamics: an evolutionary model of innovation and imitation', *Journal of Economic Behavior and Organization*, **5**: 159–90.

Iwai, K. (1984b), 'Schumpeterian dynamics, Part II. Technological progress, firm growth and economic selection', *Journal of Economic Behavior and Organization*, **5**: 321–55.

Iwai, K. (1990), 'Towards a disequilibrium theory of long run profits', *Journal of Evolutionary Economics*, **1**: 19–21.

Jacquemin, A. (1979), 'Entropy measure of diversification and corporate growth', *Journal of Industrial Economics*, **27** (4): 359–69.

Jacquemin, A. (1987), *The New Industrial Organization: Market Forces and Strategic Behavior*, Cambridge, MA: MIT Press.

Jewkes, J., D. Sawers and R. Stillerman (1969), *The Sources of Invention*, 2nd edn, New York: Norton Press.

Jovanovic, B. and G.M. MacDonald (1994a), 'Competitive Diffusion,' *Journal of Political Economy*, **102**: 24–52.

Jovanovic, B. and G.M. MacDonald (1994b), 'The life cycle of a competitive industry', *Journal of Political Economy*, **102** (2): 322–47.

Kaldor, N. (1985), *Economics without Equilibrium*, Cardiff: University College Cardiff Press.

Kalecki, M. (1945), 'On the Gibrat distribution', *Econometrica*, **13**: 161–70.

Kamien, M. and N. Schwartz (1975), 'Market structure and innovation: a survey', *Journal of Economic Literature*, **13**: 1–37.

Kamien, M. and N. Schwartz (1982), *Market Structure and Innovation*, Cambridge, MA: Cambridge University Press.

Kester, C.W. (1984), 'Today's options for tomorrow's growth', *Harvard Business Review*, **62** (2): 153–60.

Klein, B.H. (1977), *Dynamic Economics*, Cambridge, MA: Harvard University Press.

Klepper, S. (1996), 'Exit, entry, growth, and innovation over the product life-cycle', *American Economic Review*, **86** (3): 562–83.

Klepper, S. and E. Graddy (1990), 'The evolution of new industries and the determinants of market structure', *Rand Journal of Economics*, **21**: 24–44.

Klepper, S. and K. Simons (1997), 'Technological extinctions of industrial firms: an inquiry into their nature and causes', *Industrial and Corporate Change*, **6** (2): 379–460.

Koopmans, T.C. (1937), *Linear Regression Analysis of Economic Time Series*, Haarlem: De Erven F. Bohm.

Krugman, P. (1979), 'Increasing returns, monopolistic competition and international trade', *Journal of International Economics*, **9**: 469–79.

Krugman, P. (1994), *Peddling Prosperity: Economic Sense and Nonsense in the Age of Diminished Expectations*, London: Norton.

Kwasnicki, W. (1996), *Knowledge, Innovation and Economy: An Evolutionary Exploration*, Cheltenham, UK and Brookfield, VT: Edward Elgar.

Landes, D.S. (1969), *The Unbound Prometheus. Technological Change and Industrial Development in Western Europe from 1750 to the Present*, Cambridge, MA: Cambridge University Press.

Levin, R.C. (1978), 'Technical change, barriers to entry and market structure', *Economica*, **45**: 347–61.

Levin, R.C., M. Cohen, A.K. Klevorick, R.R Nelson and S. Winter (1987), 'Appropriating the returns from industrial R&D', *Brookings Papers on Economic* Activity: 783–820.

Lunn, J. (1986), 'An empirical analysis of process and product patenting: a simultaneous equation framework', *Journal of Industrial Economics*, **34**: 319–28.

Lunn, J. and M. Stephen (1986), 'Market structure, firm structure, and research and development', *Quarterly Review of Economics and Business*, **26**: 31–44.

Malerba, F. (1985), *The Semiconductor Business. The Economics of Rapid Growth and Decline*, London: Frances Pinter.

Malerba, F. and L. Orsenigo (1996), 'The dynamics and evolution of industries', *Industrial and Corporate Change*, **5** (1): 51–88.

Malkiel, B.G. and J.G. Cragg (1970), 'Expectations and the structure of share prices', *American Economic Review*, September: 601–17.

Mankiw, G., D. Romer and M. Shapiro (1985), 'An unbiased reexamination of stock market volatility', *Journal of Finance*, **40**: 677–87.

Mansfield, E. (1968), *Industrial Research and Technological Innovation – An Econometric Analysis*, New York: Norton.

Mansfield, F., M. Schwartz and S. Wagner (1981), 'Imitation costs and patents: an empirical study', *Economic Journal*, **91**: 907–18.

March, J.G. (1991), 'Exploration and exploitation in organizational learning', *Organization Science*, **2**: 71–87.

Marengo, L. (1993), 'Knowledge distribution and coordination in organizations; on some aspects of the exploitation vs. exploration trade-off', *Revue Internationale de Systemique*, **7** (5): 553–71.

Markides, C. (1998), 'Strategic innovation in established companies', *Sloan Management Review*, Spring: 31–42.

Marshall, A. (1948), *Principles of Economics*, 5th edn, London: Macmillan.

Marx, K. (1919), *Capital*, Chicago: Charles H. Kerr.

Mazzucato, M. (1998), 'A computational model of economies of scale and market share instability', *Structural Change and Economic Dynamics*, **9**: 55–83.

Mazzucato, M. and W. Semmler (1997), 'Excess volatility and market share dynamics: a simulation model', New School for Social Research, mimeo.

Mazzucato, M. and W. Semmler (1999), 'Stock market volatility and market share instability during the US automobile industry life-cycle', *Journal of Evolutionary Economics*, **9** (1): 67–96.

Metcalfe, J.S. (1994), 'Competition, Fisher's principle and increasing returns in the selection process', *Journal of Evolutionary Economics*, **4** (4): 327–46.

Mirowski, P. (1989),'The probablistic counter-revolution or how stochastic concepts came to neoclassical economic theory', *Oxford Economic Papers*, **41** (1): 217–35.

Moody's Manual of Investments (1927–95), New York: Moody's Investor Services.

Mowery, D.C. (1983), 'Industrial research and firm size, survival, and growth in American manufacturing, 1921–1946: an assessment', *Journal of Economic History*, **43**: 953–80.

Mowery, D. and N. Rosenberg (1979), 'The influence of market demand upon innovation: a critical review of some recent empirical studies', *Research Policy*, **8**: 102–53.

Mueller, D.C. (1986), *Profits in the Long Run*, New York: Cambridge University Press.

Mueller, D. (1990), 'Profits and the process of competition', in D. Mueller (ed.), *The Dynamics of Company Profits: An International Comparison*, Cambridge: Cambridge University press: pp. 1–14.

Mueller, D.C. and T.E. Tilton (1969), 'Research and development costs as a barrier to entry', *Canadian Journal of Economics*, **2** (4): 570–79.

Mukhopadhyay, A. (1985), 'Technological progress and change in the US: 1963–77', *Southern Economic Journal*, **52**: 141–9.

Nelson, R.R. (1993), *National Innovation Systems*, Oxford: Oxford University Press.

Nelson, R.R. (1995), 'Recent evolutionary theorizing about economic change', *Journal of Economic Literature*, **33** (1): 48–90.

Nelson, R.R. and S.G. Winter (1982), *An Evolutionary Theory of Economic Change*, Cambridge, MA: Harvard University Press.

Pakes, A. and R. Ericson (1987), 'Empirical implications of alternative models of firm dynamics', Social Systems Research Institute Workshop Series, University of Wisconsin.

Parker, W. (1978), *The Economics of Innovation*, 2nd edn, London: Longman.

Pavitt, K. (1984), 'Sectoral patterns of technical change: towards a taxonomy and a theory', *Research Policy*, **3**: 343–73.

Phillips, A. (1971), *Technology and Market Structure: A Study of the Aircraft Industry*, Lexington, MA: Heath Lexington Books.

Radzicki, M.J. and J.D. Sterman (1994), 'Evolutionary economics and system dynamics', in England (1994): pp. 61–89.

Rae, J.B. (1965), *The American Automobile*, Chicago: University of Chicago Press.

Rosenberg, N. (1963), 'Technological change in the machine tool industry, 1840–1910', *Journal of Economic History*, **23** (4): 414–43.

Rothblum, U. and S. Winter (1985), 'Asymptotic behavior of market shares for a stochastic growth model', *Journal of Economic Theory*, **36**: 352–66.

Rothwell, R. and M. Dodgson (1996), 'Innovation and firm size', in *The Handbook of Industrial Innovation*, Cheltenham, UK: Edward Elgar: pp. 310–24.

Ryals, S.D. (1985), 'Secular and cyclical trends in price–earnings ratios', *Business Economics*, **20** (2): 19–23.

Santa Fe Institute (1990), *Santa Fe Institute Studies on Complexity* (1990), Berlin: Springer-Verlag.

Scherer, F.M. (1965), 'Firm size, market structure, opportunity and the output of patented inventions', *American Economic Review*, **57**: 524–31.

Scherer, F.M. (1984), *Innovation and Growth: Schumpeterian Perspectives*, Cambridge, MA: MIT Press.

Scherer, F.M. and D. Ross (1990), *Industrial Market Structure and Economic Performance*, 3rd edn, Boston, MA: Houghton Mifflin.

Schmookler, S. (1966), *Invention and Economic Growth*, Cambridge, MA: Harvard University Press.

Schumacher, E.F. (1973), *Small is Beautiful*, London: Harper & Row.

Schumpeter, J. (1934), *The Theory of Economic Development*, Cambridge, MA: Harvard University Press.

Schumpeter, J. (1942), *Capitalism, Socialism and Democracy*, New York: Harper & Row.

Schuster, P. and K. Sigmund (1983), 'Replicator dynamics', *Journal of Theoretical Biology*, **100**: 533–8.

Scott, J.T. (1984), 'Firm vs. industry variables in R&D intensity', in Z. Griliches (ed.), *R&D, Patents and Productivity*, Chicago: University of Chicago Press: pp. 233–48.

Seltzer, L.H. (1973), *A Financial History of the American Automobile Industry*, Clifton, NY: Augustus M. Kelley.

Semmler, W. (1984), *Competition, Monopoly and Differential Profit Rates*, New York: Columbia University Press.

Shannon, C. and W. Weaver (1949), *The Mathematical Theory of Communication*, Nebraska: University of Illinois Press.

Shiller, R.J. (1989), *Market Volatility*, Cambridge, MA: MIT Press.

Silverberg, G. (1983), 'Embodied technical progress in a dynamic economic model: the self-organization approach', *Lecture Notes in Economics and Mathematical Systems: Non-linear Models of Fluctuating Growth*, Vol. 292, Berlin: Springer-Verlag.

Silverberg, G. (1987), 'Technical progress, capital accumulation and effective demand: a self-organization model', in D. Batten (ed.), *Economic Evolution and Structural Adjustment*, Berlin: Springer-Verlag: pp. 176–44.

Silverberg, G. (1988), 'Modelling economic dynamics and technical change: mathematical approaches to self-organization and evolution', in Dosi et al. (1988): pp. 531–59.

Silverberg, G., G. Dosi, and L. Orsenigo (1988), 'Innovation, diversity and diffusion: a self-organizing model', *Economic Journal*, **98** (393): 1032–54.

Simon, H.A. (1984), 'On the behavioral foundations of economic dynamics', *Journal of Economic Behavior and Organization*, **5** (1): 35–55.

Simon, H.A. and C.P. Bonini (1958), 'The size distribution of business firms', *American Economic Review*, **48** (4): 607–17.

Smith, A. (1937), *The Wealth of Nations*, New York: Modern Library.

Spence, M. (1981), 'The learning curve and competition', *Bell Journal of Economics*, **12**: 49–70.

Sraffa, P. (1926), *The Production of Commodities by Means of Commodities*, Cambridge, UK: Cambridge University Press.

Stigler, G. (1958), 'Economies of scale', *Journal of Law and Economics*, **1**: 54–71.

Sutton, J. (1997), 'Gibrat's legacy', *Journal of Economic Literature*, **35**: 40–59.

Sutton, J. (1998), *Technology and Market Structure*, Cambridge, MA: MIT Press.

Taylor, C.T. and Z.A. Silberston (1973), *The Economic Impact of the Patent System*, Cambridge, UK: Cambridge University Press.

Tirole, J. (1988), *The Theory of Industrial Organization*, Cambridge, MA: MIT Press.

Tushman, M.L. and P. Anderson (1986), 'Technological discontinuities and organizational environments', *Administrative Science Quarterly*, **31**: 439–65.

Walsh, V. (1984), 'Invention and innovation in the chemical industry: demand pull or discovery push?', *Research Policy*, **13**: 211–34.

Ward's Automotive Yearbook (1936–95), Detroit: Ward's Communications.

Weidlich, W. and M. Braun (1992), 'The master equation approach to nonlinear economics', *Journal of Evolutionary Economics*, **2** (3): 233–65.

Weidlich, W. and G. Haag (1982), *Concepts and Models of a Quantitative Sociology – The Dynamics of Interacting Populations*, Springer Series in Synergetics, Vol. 14, Berlin: Springer Verlag.

Weiss, L. (1963), 'Average concentration ratios and industrial performance', *Journal of Industrial Economics*, **11**: 237–54.

Williamson, O.E. (1965), 'Innovation and market structure', *Journal of Political Economy*, **73**: 67–73.

Williamson, O.E. (1985), *The Economic Institutions of Capitalism, Firms, Markets, Relational Contracting*, New York: Free Press.

Winter, S. (1984), 'Schumpeterian competition in alternative technological regimes', *Journal of Economic Behavior and Organization*, **5**: 287–320.

Winter, S. and U. Rothblum (1985), 'Asymptotic behavior of market shares for a stochastic growth model', *Journal of Economic Theory*, **36**: 352–66.

Woo, C. and A. Cooper (1982), 'The surprising case for low market share', *Harvard Review*, (November/December): 106–16.

Young, A. (1928), 'Increasing returns and economic progress', *Economic Journal*, **38**: 527–32.

Index